Silent for Sixty Years
Ben Fainer – Holocaust Survivor

Ben Fainer

&

Mark W. Leach

Dedicated to my mother

Hannah Ida Urman Fainer

This wonderful song captures the love I have in my
heart for my dear mother. May she, and all the mothers
lost in the Holocaust, rest in peace.

My Yiddishe Momme

Of things I should be thankful for I've had a goodly share.
And as I sit here in the comfort of my cozy chair,
my fancy takes me to a humble eastside tenement,
three flights up in the rear to where my childhood days were spent.
It wasn't much like Paradise but 'mid the dirt and all,
there sat the sweetest angel, one that I fondly call my yiddishe
momme. I need her more than ever now.
My yiddishe momme, I'd like to kiss that wrinkled brow.
I long to hold her hands once more as in days gone by
and ask her to forgive me for things I did that made her cry.
How few were her pleasures; she never cared for fashion's styles.
Her jewels and treasures she found them in her baby's smiles.
Oh, I know that I owe what I am today
to that dear little lady so old and gray
to that wonderful yiddishe momme of mine.

Introduction

Loss

I've played my father's story of inexplicable cruelty and unfathomable loss over and over in my head since I was a child. I struggled to keep my imagination from going into the abyss. My father's stillness screamed in its silence; I was unable to ask what happened, how he suffered, felt or survived?

My father is approaching 83 and now ready to tell his story. Like you, I will be hearing the whole ugliness for the first time.

Close your eyes and go back to your childhood. You are ten years old -- revisit your fondest memories of your mom, recall playing with your siblings or friends. Now, see armed, uniformed men force their way into your home and violently cart-off you and your family. Picture yourself placed in barracks with thousands of strangers, with no heat and only the smallest ration of food. You are alone, your family is gone, but you don't know where to. For six years your nightmare continues as you are beaten and forced to do heavy labor. You learn, your mother and your siblings were put to death in a gas chamber. Think about it. Can you even imagine?

The thoughts of the unknown, the sickening torture his infant brother, siblings and mom surely must have suffered, tore his mind and soul to pieces. Gone was the nurturing love of his mother -- always there to teach, listen and support. Never to happen again -- stolen, murdered. No more planning a simple meal, sweet birthdays, holidays, family and religious traditions. Nothing…all gone. Dad was just a little boy when all this was taken from him; taken from his family, his friends and the life he dreamed of living.

While, my siblings and I do have firsthand experience of the effects the Holocaust had on a survivor, we did not hear any stories growing up. During those years, my dad was a tortured soul. It seems he was always running away from his emotions, never experiencing his feelings. His days were spent avoiding, repressing memories. And when he slept, his mind tried to hide him from the Nazis and the nightmares he lived through. This silent wave of torture flowed through our home. My mom told each of her children about the Holocaust at different times while we grew up. We couldn't run from the truth, it remained in the serial number tattooed on my dad's arm. The wondering about the unknown horror of the invasion and the bombings haunted my sleep for many years.

I was born on the fourth of July, and grew to dislike fireworks. This past fourth, as fireworks were going off, I said to someone I barely knew in the grocery store parking lot, that I hated fireworks. It just came out, I was a little embarrassed. After asking myself for months why I said that, the answer dawned on me. Not only was my dad's way of looking at life permanently altered, his pain and fears were passed on to his children and still lives in each of us today.

Gratitude

My father has the highest respect and gratitude for our Armed Forces. Despite all the political chaos and ignorance of the 1940's, my father knows he owes his life to the men and women who rescued him and the other survivors. My dad has formed several relationships with personnel of all ranks in multiple branches of service. He travels to military bases and brings small and large groups to the Holocaust

Museum & Learning Center in St. Louis, Missouri ("Holocaust Center").

Thankfully, the Holocaust has not disappeared from our collective memory. Because the healing continues, there are many people who help the survivors during their later years, their second liberation. These people are doing wonders to help people like my dad face the pain and torture they repressed from 1945.

At the top of that list is Stephen Spielberg. Through his movies and humanitarian efforts, Spielberg opens the eyes of the world to the atrocities of the Holocaust and what the survivors somehow survived. In his goodness, he put his personal finances not into a personal exotic retreat, but into a special island where humanity can go to heal and learn from this horrific incident in history.

In 1994, Spielberg established The Shoah Foundation (now known as USC Shoah Foundation) to collect and preserve the stories of approximately 50,000 Holocaust survivors around the world. The Shoah Foundation's St. Louis emissary was Marcie Rosenberg, who met my dad about one year after my mom passed away. Initially, when Marcie approached him about making a video, he was dismissive and not interested. Marcie, however, did not take no for an answer, and she continued to ask and present her case. Eventually, Dad submitted. A healing seed was planted. Marcie has worked continuously and tirelessly, without compensation for nearly twenty years on behalf of the survivors, their families and the Holocaust Center. Had I grown up with Jewish tradition, instead of my Irish Catholic mother's beliefs, I would know the Hebrew word equivalent to a Catholic Saint. That is Marcie.

About five years ago, my dad returned to living in St. Louis and was asked to speak to a group of students at the Holocaust Center. Again, he was not interested. He had no public speaking experience, was not interested in acquiring any, or in telling his story. Once again, Marcie worked her magic, and he eventually agreed. He began speaking periodically. Over time, that increased gradually and evolved from quarterly to monthly, then weekly and then several times per week. He was well received by every audience and became a requested speaker. Paradoxically, the speaking resonated in his being, and he developed a passion, a mission in honor of the mother he lost.

A few years ago, one of my father's large speaking engagements to the military was featured in a local newspaper. Michael Staenberg, a St. Louis businessman, intrigued by the article, called my dad to arrange a meeting. Since that time, Staenberg has shown him the upmost respect and generosity. My father is so blessed to have him as a friend.

Mark Leach has spent the past year working with my father to coordinate writing this book. For Mark, I would guess this was like walking a bull on a leash. Please know, Mark, that my dad and family are grateful for your patience and perseverance in making his book a reality.

I have watched the seeds of healing slowly grow over the past 18 years. My father has told his story to thousands of students and others around the St. Louis area. While I think the process of telling his story has been therapeutic, it seems the greater healing effects have resulted from thousands of people listening to his story. The recognition, respect and admiration he has received from students, the military and professionals, along with the honorary degrees and medals, has allowed him to find himself and put some of the pieces back together. And while it is impossible to remove the effects of the damage, the daily emotional battle of repressing/erupting hurt, pain, and anger, has lessened. I feel my father's soul has been set free. For this, I, my siblings and my father are eternally grateful to all.

Sharon Hannah (Fainer) Berry

January 19, 2013

Silent for Sixty Years
Ben Fainer – Holocaust Survivor

Chapter One

Work Will Set You Free

How can I tell my story? I'm a simple tailor. I can cut and sew fabric into anything you like as easily as I can breathe. I could make you a beautiful suit in just an hour. But to put together the bits and pieces of my life, the horrible and the wonderful, is a daunting task. I'm not a storyteller, nor an educated writer. Before the Nazis came to our town in Poland, I'd completed only a few years of grade school. I was just a kid when they took us away. After six years in the camps, I had to teach myself how to speak, read, and write English. I converse with people quite well, although I still have a bit of an accent.

I wish you were here with me right now; it would be so much easier. Sitting face-to-face, I could explain it all. I could help you understand. You'd see right away that I didn't let all that happened sour me. You'd see the twinkle in my eyes and my great love of life. I'd be able to sense when the horror was getting too much for you. I'd lighten up a bit and blend in a little humor. That's how I tell my story. I'll do my best with simple words on a page. However, to be honest, I'm a little doubtful I can tell it as well.

A dear friend told me not to worry. She said that as I write this, I should pretend you and I are sitting here at my kitchen table. We're having coffee or maybe a little Scotch, and we're just chatting. We're getting comfortable, and you notice the tattoo on my arm. You say, "Ben, you've never told me about the camps. Would you mind telling me a little bit about them?" And of course I'm quite the talker. I never stop with a "little bit" of anything. If I do something, I'm in. I'm all the way in and then some.

I've thought about a lot of things over the years. I could go into great detail about the horror of the camps and the death-marches. However none of that compares with the loss of my family. When I think of the dearest thing to my heart, my mother, I die inside. She's gone and for what reason? And I think of my three siblings, including my eight-day old baby sister. For what reason are they gone? At the time I could never figure that out.

Now we know. Hitler wanted to do away with the Jews, and he did a pretty fair job. I never wanted to dwell on the horror. It's never something I talked about. Now I hear there are people claiming these things didn't happen. I never wanted to rehash all this. It's painful. It's difficult. But people need to know.

It's hard for me to make someone understand about the camps. If you haven't been through it, this may be impossible. We would stand at roll call at three o'clock in the morning, in the rain, the pouring rain, and we were starving to death and waiting to go out to another horror. The camp was one horror. The march was a different horror. It's hard to describe. I don't know what to tell you. Life was utterly terrible, yet utterly basic. This is what it is: you get up, you march, and you work. If you stop, you're dead with a bullet in your head. So you march. You march, and you work.

The cruelty was horrifying. The only way I can describe it is that I was thinking every day, "How am I going to survive this?" I would open my eyes every morning shocked to still be breathing. That was my first thought every morning for six years.

I'm sorry to tell you this; at Buchenwald I saw people being put into the crematorium ovens while they were still alive. I heard their screams for help, but what could I do? My barracks was right next to the ovens. I saw this every day. The bodies of the dead and almost-dead were stacked up all around like cord wood. The Germans couldn't burn them fast enough. There was no way these poor people could survive. They couldn't walk. They couldn't work. And if you can't stand on your feet and do what you're supposed to do, you're gone.

2

In the camps you needed to focus on a few basic things: try your best to stay healthy (in spite of the fact that you're starving to death and living in filth), don't open your mouth to anyone, and resist the ever seductive temptation to give up. I had to will myself out of the bunk in the morning and force my legs to walk. Had I failed, I would have been gone. This wasn't how life was every once in a while on occasional "bad days." This is how it was every minute, of every hour, of every day.

At many of the camps the Germans put up signs, "*Arbeit Macht Frei*," which means, "Work will set you free." And of course it was a lie. There was no free. There was work, or there was death.

Freedom was a distant yet powerful dream. The thought of it kept me going. In the camps and on the long marches, the only thing that will set you free is to make sure you stay alive. Do this every day, and someday fine American soldiers might set you free. If you don't, if you give up, you're dead. When I marched to work, on many dozens of occasions, a guy would collapse to the ground. If he didn't get up, he'd get a bullet in his head and was immediately kicked off into the ditch aside the road.

During the marches if I started to slow down, guys poked me and said, "Bendet, don't fall asleep. You fall asleep, you're gone. Don't fall down. Be strong. Keep going." They really helped me. We all helped each other as best we could.

Work did not set me free from the camps. Brave and kind American soldiers won my freedom. Their work and sacrifice set me free. I can't describe to you the great feeling it was to go, in the blink of an eye, from six years of utter terror, to joyous freedom! It's indescribable. It was like being reborn. Can you imagine? All of a sudden, after six years of fearing monsters in uniform, I was engulfed by a group of uniformed soldiers who wanted only to help me. Some of the American soldiers were Jewish and spoke Yiddish! I was being fed. I was being treated like a king!

Well of course I'm an American now. You know how Americans are. We Americans have a great heart. We're always taking care of somebody else. The soldiers who liberated me were the best of who we as a nation hope to be. I owe them everything. They were indescribable and unbelievable. My heart swells with love and pride every time I think of them.

When they rescued me I was 15. By that time I weighed only about 70 pounds. I don't know how much longer I could have kept marching. The Allies were closing in on the Germans from all directions. The Nazis didn't want them to find us and discover the evil they'd done to us. All across Germany and Poland, they were marching thousands upon thousands of us from one place to another trying to keep ahead of the advancing front lines. Deprived of gas chambers and slave labor camps, where their purpose was to work us to death, the only thing left was to march us to death. If they failed, if we survived, we could tell the world what they'd done.

And then they were there, those beautiful American tanks and soldiers! I remember it as if it happened yesterday. I was liberated on April 23, 1945, along a road outside the village of Cham, Germany. It was 10 o'clock in the morning. It was raining. Over the grass covered hill, to the right of the road, several tanks appeared. At first I thought they were German tanks. I said to myself, "This is it. After all this, they've come to kill us." Then as they got closer, even through the pouring rain, I could see they weren't German. I could see they were Americans!

I'd seen countless people die. After six seemingly endless years, I had survived. Honestly I don't know how or why. I could have died a dozen different ways during any single day in the camps. It happened all so very long ago; however it's burned deeply into my memory. At first it came back nearly every night in my dreams: the kapos, the hangings, the ovens. In my worst nightmares I'd relive watching helplessly as my mother and siblings were loaded into the back of the German truck. Sleep was difficult during those early post-war years.

Later I could go days without giving it a single thought. Then without warning, in the middle of going about my business, the hint of a certain smell or the sound of a car backfiring could send me right back, back to the horror. I worked very hard at pushing it down, keeping it locked away. For over sixty years now, I've never talked about these things. I've built a wonderful life. I've had a great marriage. I have incredible kids and grandkids. People ask, "How do you do it? How do you put it all behind and not just survive, but thrive?"

I'm not sure, but it may be that I've never considered myself a victim. My mother, my siblings, they were victims. It may also be something else. I tell you, obviously, I have no love for that son-of-a-bitch, Hitler; but, as they say, even a blind pig roots up an acorn every once in a while. So even the horrible swine, Hitler, got one little thing right. The signs, *"Arbeit Macht Frei,"* meaning "Work will set you free," were a big lie at the camps, but they were true for me thereafter. I worked harder for my wife and kids than I ever did at the camps. I worked two and three jobs, eighteen-hour days, to give my wife and kids good lives. When I wasn't at work, I doted over them during every spare moment.

And I worked hard at enjoying life: travel, good books, and good food. I work hard at squeezing every bit of juice out of life, which, yes, includes a good drink now and then. Why not? As the wise Yiddish saying goes, "A man comes from the dust and in the dust he will end, and in the mean time it is good to drink vodka!" So no thanks to Hitler and his lousy signs, work has set me free.

Chapter Two

A Crack in the Silence

For all those years I kept my mouth shut, and I worked. Every once in a while, if I wasn't careful, a guy at work would notice the tattoo on my forearm. It was hot in the cutting room, and being focused on my work, I might forget and push up my sleeves. Then I'd hear, "Ben, were you in the Holocaust? Were you in a concentration camp?" I'd push my sleeves back down to cover it up. If I liked the guy, I'd make up a little joke about needing to write my phone number on my arm so I wouldn't forget it or other such nonsense. Then I'd change the subject. If I didn't like the guy, I'd just tell him to mind his own business. Either way the guys I worked with got the message.

That's how it was. People would know me; they might know all kinds of things about me: my wife, my kids, my favorite restaurant. However they wouldn't know about my past. I'm not a psychiatrist. I'm sure there are all kinds of complicated ways to explain it. All I know is that I didn't want to dwell on it. I simply wanted to take care of my family, and talking about my past didn't put food on the table.

That's how I lived for over 60 years. Then a number of years ago when I was about 75, after my dear wife passed away, I moved to Florida. I'm an outgoing guy, and I got to know this rabbi. His name

6

is Mendel. He invited me several times out to dinner. And of course I never talked about my past back in Germany and Poland. One day we were sitting down at his home, and you know some of the rabbis like a drink, and his wife was in a different room with the kids, and we were enjoying a drink, and I said, "Rabbi, I would like you to do me a favor."

He said, "What would you like?"

"I would like for you to Bar Mitzvah me."

He set down his drink and said, "Ben, you're joking?"

I said, "No, Rabbi. I'm not joking. When I was 13, I was in Buchenwald. So I've never had a Bar Mitzvah."

"Why didn't you tell me this before?" He was totally flabbergasted, and he told me, "It would be a joy to my heart!"

But I had a little problem. You have to read a passage of the Torah in Hebrew during a Bar Mitzvah. I had studied a little Hebrew before the camps, but it was all gone from my head. I tried very hard to study, but I wasn't making much progress. I was worried because I really wanted to have a Bar Mitzvah. I wrestled with it for a while, but I just couldn't do it. Reluctantly I met with the rabbi and told him, "Just forget it, Rabbi. I can't do it."

Rabbi was so kind. He said, "Ben, quit studying. I have a remedy for you. Strictly speaking, what I'm proposing is against God's law. However I believe the Almighty God will not mind if I do this for you. I will write out how the Hebrew words sound in English. You'll have no problem."

So I had a Bar Mitzvah, and there were about 150 people there. It was a great moment. But I didn't know the rabbi had invited the press. There were reporters from all over the area, including West Palm Beach, Miami, and Boca Raton.

The next day there was an article in the local newspaper with a photograph of the rabbi and me. It talked all about my time in the camps. I was sitting at my kitchen table, and I almost spilled my coffee. Out loud, to my Golden Retriever, D.J., I said, "*Oy gavalt*, what the hell did my rabbi do to me?" Now everyone would know: my neighbors, the guys at the gym, the waitress at the deli. Would they treat me differently? Would they ask me questions? I wasn't prepared for this. I had just wanted a nice quiet Bar Mitzvah.

About a week later I was at home reading the paper; the TV was on with Tom Brokaw doing the evening news. D.J. was resting his head across my knee, and the phone rang. I picked it up, and a male voice asked, "May I speak to Mr. Bernard Fainer?"

I said, "This is he."

The guy on the phone said, "My name is Norris Nims. I happened to pick up the paper where it says, 'Holocaust Survivor Bar Mitzvahed.' It says you were liberated in Cham, Germany. I think I was there. I think I was one of the soldiers who liberated you."

I said, "Sir, are you joking? You must be joking. You couldn't have liberated me."

"Yes I did. I was there. That's the reason I'm calling you. It was at 10 o'clock in the morning on April 23, 1945, in Cham, Germany. It was raining."

And I said, "Tell me the truth. You're not joking are you? Because I think I just went doo-doo in my pants, and I think you're giving me a heart attack!" Forgive me, but I sometimes say things like that.

I asked him, "Where do you live?

"In Wellington right off 441."

"I know where you are. I'm five minutes from you!"

He gave me directions to his house. I grabbed my keys, snapped the leash on D.J., and off we went. A few minutes later I stood before his front door. I rang the bell. I was excited and a little nervous. Then the door opened, and he was there: tall and skinny as a fiddle. He was an older man, but he looked to be in good health. He had bright eyes and a warm smile. I liked him immediately.

We shook hands, formally, as men often do. Then, without thought or hesitation, we hugged for a moment in silence. Men of our generation are not generally big huggers, but Norris and I had shared something unique and powerful in our distant past. We'd each been through our own version of hell before coming together during that victorious spring of 1945. He searched my face very closely for a moment and said, "I may have met you during the liberation, but I don't remember." I said very much the same thing.

This is not surprising. I was 15, and Norris had been in his thirties. There were hundreds of American soldiers and thousands of survivors who converged in the pouring rain. Our column of prisoners may have stretched out for over a mile along that road. I didn't speak a word of English. I hugged and kissed the hands of a lot of soldiers, but I could only speak with the few who knew Yiddish. Norris might have handed me food and water, but with all the commotion and all the years, how could we remember?

We sat down and started to chat. At first we stuck with safe topics, such as careers and family. After a time the conversation began to lag. Norris and I were complete strangers bound only by a profound experience: an experience neither of us had discussed with anyone for over 60 years. We'd run out of small talk, and yet we were hesitant to broach the single topic that had brought us together. I can't remember exactly who got it started. Maybe it was Norris. Perhaps he asked me about my health, saying something about how healthy I looked. He said he couldn't believe it because we all looked so pitiful back in Cham. Once we got going though, it all started spilling out. It was painful, a bit exhausting, but overall left me feeling deeply satisfied. It had finally come out after all those years.

Oh, I tell you something, the guy is an unbelievable man! He's an unbelievable fella! We became great friends. From then on Norris and I talked on the phone nearly every day. I'd have him over to my place, and I'd cook a little dinner. After dinner we'd bend our elbows together, you know, have some drinks and talk. Norris didn't like Scotch; he preferred a cold beer. Over time we grew to love each other like brothers.

Life is funny that way. I'm ever astounded by such things. If you don't believe in God, then these things happen for no good reason. The paths of two men just happen to cross along a road in Germany. They happen to cross again decades later in a small community in Florida – for no reason. These are simply random occurrences. I think if you live long enough, and experience enough of them, you start to believe there's a little more to it than that. People and places may seem meaningless at one time, but then years later reappear with startling meaning. Over time I've grown to see life as an intricate fabric woven with great care, interlaced with profoundly meaningful threads tying people and places together across time.

But I'm not here to preach. I'm here to tell my story. In regard to my friendship with Norris, I like to think of an old Jewish expression. It's a little clearer in Yiddish than in English. The best I can do is put it this way, "Two mountains from two different sides of the world can never get together. But two humans can." That's basically what it means.

9

Chapter Three

My Childhood

Where do you want me to start, from the beginning in Poland? Life wasn't easy. We had no money. In winter sometimes it would get down to 25 below. Now people love to go on about wind chill. Back then we didn't bother with such nonsense. The Polish winters were brutally cold with or without wind.

I'm from the small city of Bedzin, very near Poland's border with Germany. We lived in a humongous apartment complex called Modrizejowska 77. Modrizejowska was the main street through Bedzin: cobblestone and jam-packed with apartments and shops. Our building's street number was 77, which was posted on a metal sign next to the large arch entrance from the street. Many tenants worked in the garment industry. Some, like my father, ran small businesses out of their dwellings. The archway from the street was broad, wide enough to accommodate the constant flow of people pushing carts laden with bolts of cloth, food from the market, and small children. This entrance was a great funnel of people, noise, and the cold Polish winter wind.

The archway itself was built into a street-facing apartment building and opened into a cobblestone courtyard about half the size of a football field. The courtyard was surrounded by plain looking, three-story cinder-block apartment buildings. We lived on the first floor of the building on the left side of the courtyard. Some of my relatives lived in the building on the right. There were three large, low wooden outhouses in front of the row of apartments to the rear of the court-yard; there were no indoor bathroom facilities. Two of the outhouses were for men and one for women. Each outhouse was large enough to seat eight to ten people sitting along a sturdy wooden bench. The courtyard smelled quite a bit better in the wintertime. This may have been the only good thing about the long Polish winters!

We had no running water. Starting when I was about six and a half, my chore was to fetch water for my mother, so she could cook, do our laundry, and things like that. I would carry two buckets, each hung from the end of a wooden pole across my back. It was like those things you see in Africa. I think it's called a yoke. Once in the morning and once in the evening, I had to carry the water quite a ways, maybe as far as a half mile or so.

In the morning I went to Hebrew school. Then in the afternoon I went to regular school. I only attended three grades in school from the time I was born until the time I was taken away. But as the Yiddish saying goes, "One mother achieves more than a hundred teachers." And God blessed me with quite a mother. Her name was Hannah Ida Urman Fainer. With her guidance and hard work, I knew enough. I simply can't say too many good things about my dear mother. My father, on the other hand, was a different story.

His name was Rubin Fainer. You might as well know he wasn't such a great father, and he wasn't too great of a husband either. He was a tailor: a very fine tailor. However he drank all the money he earned and messed around with strange women. Sometimes he broke up all our furniture. Also he hit my mother, and he hit us. We never knew when he might blow up, so we tried to avoid him as much as possible. Learning how to deal with my father provided me with skills that later proved useful in avoiding trouble from SS men and kapos. This was my father's single contribution to my upbringing.

I don't know how I survived. I felt that I had a good God watching over me and the devil kicking me in the ass. I suppose in a similar sense, at home I had a good mother watching over me and a devil of a father kicking me in the ass.

My father couldn't read, nor write. And he couldn't tell one color from another. But in spite of these limitations, and in spite of his

11

heavy drinking, he was an excellent craftsman when it came to tailoring. He knew his business. And he was a big man, well over six feet tall and almost 300 pounds. His father also was a tailor and a big man. So my father wasn't the greatest guy in the world. I'd leave him out of the story if I could. But like a bad penny, he tended to keep popping up now and again; reluctantly I include him where I must.

But we did have the greatest mother in the world! I remember when I was little, and I'd come in freezing from fetching water. My mother would hold me and warm me with a big bear hug. It was the warmest, safest feeling in the whole world. Later in the camps or during the marches, exhausted and terrified, my thoughts would drift back to her hugs. For a moment I'd be right back there, a little boy with snow on my clothes, in the warm embrace of my loving mother. It fed my soul; it kept me going. I have no words to adequately describe her.

She was very kind, and she worked so very hard every day, not just to provide food and clothing, but also to help us with homework. She encouraged me quite a bit, always telling me that if I studied hard, maybe someday I'd become a rabbi.

My mother's father was a rabbi. I've been told there were 14 generations of rabbis in her family. I only have a little memory of my mother's father. Of course he had a beard and long side-curls just as you see observant rabbis in photos and in the movies. He was a serious man, but a kind man. Sometimes when he came around he would slip me a *zolter*; that's a 50-cent piece, which we really needed because my dad drank his money. I could tell my grandfather didn't like my father, but what could he do? I think my mother wanted more than anything for me to follow in her family tradition and become a rabbi. We were very tight on money, but she worked extra jobs to pay for me to go to Hebrew School.

There were five of us, well, six during our final week. We all squeezed into our small three-room apartment. The largest room served as both our kitchen and my father's tailor workshop. There was an oven in the kitchen where my mother cooked our meals, as well as a small wooden table where we ate. The rest of the room held my father's tailor shop. It included a long table used for cutting cloth and four or five smaller desks with sewing machines.

He may not have been such a great father, but I can tell you he was an excellent tailor. My father took orders from a few of the clothing stores in town. When he had big orders, he'd have five or six employees working in the shop. Most days there were only three or four. The chorus of sounds coming from my father's shop filled the apartment from early morning until early evening. The humming, clacking, and thumping of the busy shop made me feel safe. You see, when there were no orders my father did a lot of heavy drinking. We prayed for big orders.

We actually had two ovens in our kitchen. One was a cast-iron stove my mother used for cooking. The other was a *kachenofen*, a type of masonry heater, which served as our main source of heat. It had an opening in the bottom where we put coal or wood. Once it was warmed up, the tiles would throw the heat throughout the apartment. We mainly used wood, as coal was usually too expensive. There was a smaller, similar oven in our bedroom. Even when it was freezing outside, it was quite warm in our home.

Sometimes when we had a little money, my mother made a steaming pot of Hungarian goulash. It was wonderful! The rich smell filled the whole apartment. I could even smell it on my clothes while I was at school. Throughout the day I'd put my nose to my sleeve to take in the delicious smell. On those days I couldn't wait to get home. I knew the goulash would be waiting.

My mother was an observant Orthodox Jew, so she of course kept a kosher kitchen. Thus, although we were poor, she had two separate sets of pots, dishes, and utensils: one for meat and the other for dairy.

On Sabbath, marked by the setting of the sun on Friday, we could do no work of any kind. In preparation for the Sabbath, my mother cooked a large pot of stew, which we'd carry to the local bakery at about three in the afternoon. For a small fee the bakery held Sabbath meals in ovens for the observant Jews. After sundown on Saturday the Sabbath was over, and we'd pick up the stew from the bakery. I loved helping my mother pick up the stew. The wonderful smell of baked goods, blended with the delicious aroma of dozens of home-made stews was incredible!

The Sabbath was God's prescribed day of rest. The rules governing what constitutes work on the Sabbath have become quite complicated and minutely specific. Great rabbinical scholars have dedicated entire books to the topic. For instance we were able to add a little wood to the tile oven to keep the apartment from becoming too cold. However we could not use the cast-iron stove for cooking.

The Sabbath also gave us a little break from our father. He was gone a lot anyway, but he always headed out to God knows where on the Sabbath. I've never read the rabbinical writings governing the Sabbath; however, I'm confident they unanimously forbid going on a drinking binge and cavorting with strange women. Apparently my father hadn't read them either.

As an observant Jew my mother kept her head shaved and wore a wig. I'm not sure why this was done, but it was the practice of all the Orthodox married women. I never saw my mother without her wig, but I knew it was the custom. I never saw my mother without a scarf upon her head. This too was expected of modest Jewish women.

I was the oldest in the family. Majer, my brother, was one year younger and small for his age. He had a good heart and a funny sense of humor. In good weather we liked to play soccer together down in the courtyard (as far away from the outhouses as possible). In bad weather we played games inside. He liked to build things with his set of wooden blocks. Sometimes we'd go sledding down a small hill a short distance from our apartment. Majer sat in front of me on the little sled my mother used for pulling things home from the market. I'd push with all my might, before jumping on behind him. We'd fly down the hill laughing and hollering all the way to the bottom. It was great fun! "Bendet, let's do it again! Let's do it again," he'd shout after every run. We were very close.

I was two years older than my little sister Rosie. She looked like my father; but, like Majer and me, she had my mother's good nature. Rosie was a bit quiet, preferring mostly to keep to herself, often playing with a rag-doll my mother made for her. However Majer and I gave her plenty of attention. We loved to make her laugh. There's extra joy in seeing a naturally somber person break out in a great belly laugh!

And there was our baby sister. She was taken before she was even old enough to receive her name. By Jewish tradition a newborn is not given a name until he or she is eight days old. This is normally done at the first public gathering at the synagogue, such as the next reading of the Torah. Our poor baby sister was just eight days old when the Nazis came. There are no photos of her. Sadly, as hard as I try, I can't picture her face.

Majer slept by himself in a tiny bedroom. Everyone else slept in the larger bedroom, the one with the tile oven. There were no windows in the bedrooms, just a couple in the workshop overlooking the courtyard.

Only one photograph of the three of us survived. It is small and the edges are well worn, but the image remains clear. Rosie has a bow atop her beautiful hair. Her eyes shine brightly, though her expression is solemn. In fact, all three of us look solemn. Perhaps serious expressions were fashionable in photography at that time. I don't know. However, given all that was soon to happen, it is incredibly appropriate and more than a little prophetic.

I have no memory of this photograph being taken. It was quite an unusual event though, as we simply didn't have money to spend on such luxuries. My mother had the photograph taken, and then mailed it to her sister Ida in Dublin, Ireland. Ida, like several of my mother's siblings, fled Poland in the years leading up to the trouble. This is how the photograph survived. Other than my words, it is the only evidence that remains showing that little Majer and Rosie were real children who once lived in a small town in Poland.

I think it must have been taken sometime during the spring or summer before the trouble started. I was just a kid and knew little or nothing about what the adults were undoubtedly discussing, such as the possibility of a German invasion. Did my mother sense things might go very badly? Did she save up some of her money from scrubbing floors every week to have the photograph taken and pay for the postage to Dublin? Had my aunts and uncles, who'd long since fled Poland, tried to persuade my mother to do the same? But that would have been impossible. My father would never have left his business and drinking buddies. Perhaps sending the photograph was the closest my mother could come to getting us out.

I have no photographs of my mother. This breaks my heart. I would have loved to include her photograph in this book. I have several photos of my father. I did not include any of them. It just didn't seem right.

We lived in the town of Bedzin, which I've read is the oldest town in all of Poland. It first appears in ancient records as early as 1301. Historians believe it is even older, perhaps going all the way back to sometime in the 9th century. It had its own stone castle, which was nearly falling apart while I was a kid. They've fixed it up since then. You can go see it. They say it's really quite something. I've never been back to Poland, so I only know what I've read. I don't have anything against Poland, mind you. It's simply that it's a very big world with a lot of interesting places I haven't seen. Poland, I've seen.

Apparently the castle was originally a wooden fort, which was destroyed during an invasion in 1242. I tell you, Poland was always being invaded by someone or another. Not that it was so special, but rather it was always stuck between great powers.

After the wooden fort was burned down, they rebuilt another wooden fort and eventually replaced it with a giant stone castle about a hundred years later. Poles are like that. You can knock us down, but we stand right back up. We're naturally tough and incredibly stubborn.

Bedzin was not far from the border between Germany and Poland. When I was growing up about 22,000 Jews lived there. The Jewish community in Bedzin was very, very close.

Poland was pretty anti-Semitic. They used to call us a word that meant leper. When I was on my way to school, I'd hear, "You're a lousy Jew." I didn't know why they hated us. I don't think I ever asked anyone about it. It was just a fact of life. I remember hearing Jews had been living in Bedzin since the 1,300s. You'd think they would have gotten used to us. But maybe having to live with their hatred is why our Jewish community was so close. People took care of each other. If you needed something, you got it.

Between the Fainers and the Urmans, I had over 250 relatives living in and around Bedzin. When my father didn't drink up all the money, he'd give a little to my mother. When he didn't give her money, she'd scrub floors for people. Then I'd go with my mother to the market. In warm weather, when I was very young, she'd pull me in a small cart. In the winter, a little sled. But everywhere we went, coming to and from the market, we'd always see relatives. Today people hold giant family reunions because everyone's so spread out and so busy; they have to hold a big party so people can see each other. It wasn't that way in Bedzin. You saw everyone all the time.

My mother insisted that we were clean and our clothing was in good repair. She worked hard to make sure we didn't look as poor as we were. She scrubbed floors and scrubbed us.

I was just a kid. I was only nine and a half when the real trouble started. I didn't know who Hitler was. By the time the trouble was over, I was 15 ½. It was only then that I started to learn a little about who he was. It was only then, when I travelled all across Germany looking for my relatives, that I learned what he'd done. Of the over 250 Fainers and Urmans from my town, only two survived. I can still see their faces, the faces of all those who were lost. Lost isn't right. Let's not sugar-coat this, they were killed – murdered.

Chapter Four

The Germans

When I was seven years old we got a dog. He was a big German shepherd we named Rex. I loved that dog. I still love dogs. Before the German invasion my father was drafted into the Polish army, and he gave Rex away to somebody who lived 15 miles away.

Very soon my father came back from fighting the Germans. I remember seeing him outside the apartment shooting up at the Messerschmitt planes roaring overhead. It's no wonder why the Germans rolled over Poland so quickly. Our best defense was my lousy father, the illiterate, color-blind, drunken tailor shooting at airplanes with an old rifle left over from the First World War!

I'm standing in the doorway to our apartment building. And there's my father shooting at the sky, and I look down and up walks Rex! I couldn't believe it. I don't know how he found us, but he came right to the door. I was so happy to see him. That must have been such a strange sight: planes roaring over head, my father firing away, and I'm oblivious to it all. I'm just kneeling down hugging my dog. It wasn't a long reunion though. I had no way of knowing my life was about to change.

People called Nazis were coming. I'd never heard of them. They didn't know anything about me. But for some reason, they hated me. They hated everyone around me. To them we were less than human. My whole life, while I'd been minding my own business, going to school, playing with my siblings, helping my mother with chores, a man named Hitler had been plotting and planning to do away with us. What did I know of such things? I was just a kid. Even with planes flying right above our courtyard, I was just happy to see my dog.

The trouble started on the morning of September 4, 1939, just three days after the start of World War II. It was before dawn, maybe a little before six o'clock. We'd been awake for quite a while doing our chores and looking forward to a little breakfast. My father and five of his employees were already busy working on an order in his shop.

Rex, who was usually pretty quiet, started in with this long, low growl. I think my father was just starting to tell him to shut up, when he was interrupted by a loud rumble from outside. It was not the sound of airplanes. It was deeper in tone and closer, much closer. I ran to the window, followed by my mother and father. My heart raced as I saw six German army trucks pulling into the courtyard below. Rex started barking wildly. I couldn't believe my eyes! German soldiers jumped out of the trucks and immediately ran up the front steps of the apartment buildings all around the square.

I looked to my mother, then to my father. I didn't know what to do. Seconds later there was a violent bang at the door. A gruff voice was booming from the other side, shouting "*Raus, raus!*" My mother picked up the baby. My father ran across the room, bumping into one of the sewing tables, and sending one of his precious sewing machines to the floor. I remember thinking, "I'm glad I didn't knock his machine over like that!" because my father would have killed me. He cursed, but didn't stop to worry about his machine. He hurried straight to the door and opened it.

A large German soldier pointed a pistol at my father and yelled, "*Raus, raus!*" Rex growled and started moving toward the soldier. Without hesitation the soldier shot Rex in the head. Rex fell to the floor dead. His blood began spilling out all over my mother's spotless floor. I couldn't believe what was happening. That man just killed my dog! I wanted to take his gun and kill him, but you know that wouldn't have been very smart. As I'd soon see, if you didn't do exactly

19

what the Germans told you, you'd end up a dead duck – sometimes even if you did exactly what they told you to do.

The soldier swung the pistol around the room and then pointed to the door. My mother told me to hold the hands of my brother and sister. I grabbed Majer's hand with one and Rosie's in the other. Next Mother told us to follow my father. She motioned for him to head out into the hall. He did as he was told. I went next, my hands tightly holding onto Majer's and Rosie's. My mother, with the baby held close, followed up the rear. I suppose my father's employees left last.

The hallway was clogged by a throng of neighbors. Everyone was frightened; many were crying, and some young children were screaming. Looks of shock and utter terror hung on all the adults' faces. This scared me more than anything. I thought about turning to see my mother's face, to see if she too was terrified. But I was caught in the flow of people down the stairs. There was no way I could look back. I think someone on the floor above refused to open the door because I heard a loud crash, like a door being busted in. Crammed together we made our way out the front door and down the front steps to the courtyard. The sun wasn't up, but I could see pretty well through the harsh headlights of the trucks.

Soldiers were yelling in German and pointing, aided by a couple interpreters doing their best to make us understand. Immediately several of the soldiers approached us. Without hesitation they pulled my mother, who was holding the baby close to her chest, away to the left. Majer and Rosie were ripped from my grasp and also taken off to the left. What could I do? I had to let go.

A soldier looked at me and grunted something in German. An interpreter standing next to him said to me in Polish "Age? How old are you?" I was big for my age, something I got from my father and his father. I don't know how I knew to lie. I'd noticed that the Germans were separating us into three groups: the mothers with small children were sent to the left, the old people were sent to the center, and the men and young men were sent to the right. Somehow I knew that I had to go to the right. I can't really explain how I knew because I really didn't know what the hell was going on. But I blurted out, "Fifteen and a half." That simple lie saved my life.

My father and I stood among the other men and young men off to the right of the courtyard. I watched as more and more families were taken out of apartment buildings and divided among the three groups.

If someone didn't move fast enough, a soldier would strike them in the back or back of the head with the butt of his rifle. The blow wouldn't be hard enough to seriously injure the person, but was hard enough for everyone to get the message. This went on for about an hour, and gradually it was getting light out. Thankfully it was only September, so it wasn't cold outside. It was maybe around 50 degrees and cloudy, very cloudy.

I could see my mother and siblings across the courtyard. Every once in a while, I'd sneak a little wave to them, and they'd wave back. My mother was being very strong, I'm sure because she didn't want us to worry. Some people were really losing it. You know, crying and screaming, but not my mother. She'd been standing for over an hour holding her baby. And remember, she'd just given birth only eight days earlier. Childbirth wasn't easy in Poland back in those days. You didn't go to a fancy hospital and all that. She had a midwife, one of the ladies who helped with childbirth, come to the apartment. There was no doctor and no hospital. I'm sure she was in quite a bit of pain. Can you imagine?

On this day, the day she should have been giving her infant a name, my mother's world was being ripped apart. If I close my eyes, I can see her standing there holding the baby. In the midst of all that was so wrong, Mother stood straight and calm.

Majer looked scared, but he wasn't crying. I wonder if he felt sorry for me since I was with our father. We'd spent our entire child-hood perfecting the art of avoiding him. Just this once it turned out to be safer to be with father, than with mother. Rosie cried and clung to my mother. At first she cried loudly, her whole body writhing with sobs. Over time she became very quiet.

Next the Germans began loading the women and small children into one of the army trucks. These were large trucks with tall wooden sides and canvas tops. Before I knew it my mother, baby sister, Majer, and Rosie were loaded onto a truck. Once it was full it immediately pulled away, drove through the archway, and made a right onto Modrizejowska Street.

I stood there by my father. He just kept his head down staring at the cobblestones. I had been able to see my mother and siblings as they were loaded on the truck, but only their backs. I couldn't see their faces. And once they were on the truck, I couldn't see them at all. At the time I didn't know it was the last time I'd ever see them. I think I'm glad that I couldn't see their faces. It was bad enough seeing them only from behind. I like to remember them the way they were in normal life. I like to remember my mother being kind and strong. That's how she was.

I didn't know where they were being taken, and I didn't bother asking my father. I'm sure people around me were murmuring things about it, but the noise of all that was going on was deafening. Everything was so crazy, and I was just a kid. And though I was with my father, I felt utterly alone.

Chapter Five

Jeleśnia Forced Labor Camp

My father and I stood among the men and watched as truck after truck pulled up to the women and children group and the elderly group. As soon as a truck was full, soldiers swung up the back gate, and off it went. Just as quick another truck would pull up in its place, and the soldiers would begin forcing people onto it.

As the last of the other two groups were being loaded, a truck pulled up in front of our group. I watched as the first truck was loaded and left, which was immediately followed by a second.

Upon the arrival of the third truck, it was our turn. The soldiers pointed at us and yelled, "Go! Go! Git!" and we were prodded toward the truck. My father climbed up ahead of me using the short metal ladder built under the back gate of the truck. As I put a foot onto the ladder, my father reached down and gave me a hand up. In the midst of all that was going on, I was very surprised by this simple act of kindness. I remember thinking, "Ah, somewhere deep inside him he understands that he's a father, and I'm his son." It wasn't a big change of his heart or anything. He didn't rise to the occasion and become a real father. Sadly this simple act of helping me up into the German truck was the only fatherly thing he ever did.

23

The wooden benches that ran along each side of the truck were about 3/4s full by the time I climbed on board. My father and I found a place along the right and sat down. Once the benches were full, still more people were herded in and made to sit on the floor.

I brought with me only what I had on my back. I hadn't had anything to eat, but food was the least of my concerns. I didn't know what was going on, so finally I asked my father, "Why are we here?"

He said, "Hitler wants to do away with us. Eventually we will all be gone."

I had more questions, but I didn't ask them. I didn't understand what he was saying. I thought he meant Hitler wanted to move us someplace else and wondered, where is Hitler taking us? My father wasn't a big talker to begin with, and how could he have explained it anyway? I was just a kid. I didn't even know who Hitler was.

Under normal circumstances I would have been thrilled to ride in a truck. Of course I'd seen trucks, but I'd never ridden in one. Other than riding on my mother's little cart or sled on our way to market as a small boy, I'd gotten everywhere on my own two feet. Just one day earlier, had someone asked me if I'd like to ride on a truck, I would have jumped at the chance. It would have been amazing. On this day, however, the thrill was lost in the terror. There was nothing amazing about it.

During the ride the Germans never explained a thing. They didn't tell us where we were going. I hoped that maybe we'd meet up with my mother and siblings. But, as much as I wanted that to be true, my gut told me otherwise. For one thing, why would they take the time to separate us, if we were all going to the same place? Also the truck my mother and siblings were on had made a right onto Modrizejowska. Our truck made a left, so again, ending up in the same place didn't look likely.

I could see out the back over the top of the gate. There were other trucks following as far as the eye could see. I remember seeing the last buildings of Bedzin give way to farmland. It was the first time I'd ever seen the countryside around Bedzin. I'd lived my entire life in a small area around our apartment. Modrizejowska was a wide street, with broad sidewalks. However the buildings along both sides were built one against another. They shared walls without open spaces or alleys in between. Everything was very closed in. I was accustomed to the hustle and bustle of our crowded little neighborhood. I was comforted by it. As I looked out through the back gate at the open farmland, I remember wondering if I'd ever see my hometown again. I felt very lost in the openness.

I was the youngest on the truck. Of course I recognized faces, but I didn't know any of the men personally. Remember I was just a kid. Kids knew kids, but we didn't really talk a lot with adults. I'm sure my father knew some of them because a lot of men in 77 Modrizejowska worked in the garment industry.

There were no German soldiers in the truck with us; thus many of the men quietly discussed what they thought might happen to us. But no one knew. I was scared and worried, and I could tell the others were too. Even so everyone was pretty cooperative. I gave up my seat to one of the men sitting on the floor. Others did the same even though the hard wooden benches weren't much better.

After a long while the truck pulled off to the side and stopped. We were told to get out and head out into a field. I didn't know what was going to happen, but I was afraid it wasn't going to be good. Would they shoot us as the soldier had shot my dog Rex? I looked at their guns and pushed the image of Rex, dead on my mother's clean floor, from my mind. I looked around wanting to run, but it was all open fields dotted here and there by patches of woods and little farm houses. The woods were too far. Running would have been suicide. There was nothing I could do.

A soldier yelled something in German that I couldn't understand. I was relieved when another soldier said something while mimicking the act of going to the bathroom. The other soldiers got a big laugh and also started mimicking going to the bathroom. We were happy to learn this was a bathroom stop, rather than place to get a bullet in the head. But of course we didn't join in the laughter. We did our business and got back in the truck as fast as we could. We wanted to get back in the truck, away from the soldiers and their guns.

Once we were all on board, they closed the truck's gate. I could see the back of one of the soldiers, through the opening above the gate, as he took care of his own business. He looked very awkward trying to manage things with one hand, while holding his rifle with the other. Up to this point, the soldiers had looked invulnerable with their spotless uniforms and shiny helmets. It gave me one tiny speck of comfort to see they were not superhuman. Underneath the uniforms they were just men. That impression turned out to be quite right for these regular soldiers, the men of the *Wehrmacht*. This would not be the case later on when we encountered the men of the SS. They were not normal men underneath.

We pulled back into the long line of passing trucks. The rest of the truck ride was pretty uneventful. We made another bathroom stop later on, but it was just like the first. As I mentioned, I'd never ridden in a car or truck before. Believe it or not, I'd never been further than about a mile from our home. The vast majority of my life had existed in an area of no more than a few blocks from Modrizejowska77.

These trucks had normal diesel engines. Later, as the war wore on and petroleum became scarce, all the German trucks I saw were powered by large wood-burning furnaces attached to their sides. I've read that about 500 such wood-powered vehicles were in use in Germany by war's end. Of course, at the time, none of this mattered to me. All that mattered was staying alive.

After we'd been on the road again for about two hours, the truck stopped again. We were told to get out. I knew this wasn't another bathroom break because all the trucks were stopping and unloading. We were in a huge open area in front of row after row of long wooden barracks. I didn't know what it was, but I soon learned it was Jeleśnia, a make-shift forced labor camp. It's not listed in any of the books, nor have I found any of the experts who know of the forced labor camp at Jeleśnia.

I think this is because the Germans had crossed into Poland only days before. It would be several weeks before they'd fully subdue our nation. Then it would take the Germans a while to construct ghettos, concentration camps, and death camps. Since the round-up of people from our town was conducted so early into the war, the Germans had to make the best use of whatever places they could find. Why the Germans decided to take their first step down what became the most infamous genocide campaign in the history of the world with our little section of apartments, remains a mystery.

We were made to form a line. One by one they checked each of us into the camp. My father was just ahead of me in the line. When he got to the front, a German soldier asked him in broken Polish for his name, address, and profession. The soldier wrote in a notebook, said, "Barracks #12" and pointed for my father to head over to a small group of men off to the side.

Then I was at the front of the line; it was my turn. First he asked my age, and again I lied saying I was 15 ½. He asked me my name, address, and profession. I told him the truth, saying I was a student. He assigned me to Barracks #12.

I kept looking as more and more trucks pulled up and unloaded, hoping there might be some women and children – hoping beyond hope that one might contain my mother and siblings. But all just contained men and young men. I noticed that I was the youngest of all the people. This made me scared. Somehow I understood that it wasn't safe to stick out, to get noticed. I sized up the men in our group and stood near a couple of the shortest. I hoped this would help me to blend in.

Once enough men had been assigned to our group, about 150-200, a German soldier marched us down the long rows of buildings to my new home, Barracks #12.

Barracks #12 was exactly like all the other buildings: long, narrow wooden buildings with few windows and no plumbing. At this point we each had our own bunk. I was assigned a top bunk, with my father in the bunk below.

We were ordered to stay put. Everything was mostly quiet in the barracks. I think everyone was exhausted and in shock from all that had happened that day. Admittedly I too was in shock. I mean, one minute you're a kid doing your chores, looking forward to a little breakfast, and seeing your friends at school. The next, your family has been ripped apart, you're standing in a strange building holding a thin wool blanket, and wondering what's going to happen next.

After a long while the soldiers yelled for us to come outside. They didn't speak Polish, and we didn't speak German, but by now we knew fairly well what they wanted. They'd brought out some enormous metal pots, and we were formed into a long line. After about 30-45 minutes I reached the front of the line, where I received a small bowl of what today I would call "shit." Excuse my language, but I don't think there's any better way to put it. It was some sort of foul watery broth containing a few mushy vegetables.

I ate it. From what I could tell it looked like I was going to be here quite a while, so I knew I couldn't be picky. Even though I hadn't eaten all day, it still tasted like garbage. Had I known just how bad things would get later on, I would have been very excited about that first bowl of slop!

The area immediately around the barracks was bare and open. There were no barbed wire fences, nor guard towers. The guards made it clear that if we wandered away from the barracks, we'd be shot without warning. No one wandered. Around the perimeter of the camp, armed German soldiers walked at regular intervals just to make sure. Beyond the camp I could see farmland and patches of woods.

Not much happened for the first couple days; they were still unloading and assigning people to barracks. The day after the trucks stopped coming, the men were marched off to work in a number of shops that surrounded the camp. It was all very organized. They only had to march about a block, maybe a block and a half. They'd spend all day making machine parts, army boots, and uniforms. My father and a host of other tailors went off to a building to make German uniforms.

Perhaps that's why they started with our apartments. It could be that they badly needed uniforms and had learned from Polish officials about the large garment district in Bedzin. They scooped us up, plopped us down in a newly conquered Polish army base, and got us right to work. They may have gathered up all the sewing machines in Bedzin, along with its tailors. If nothing else, the Germans were efficient. Sadly, of course, they had no use for the elderly, women, and children of Bedzin.

I guess since I was the youngest, I didn't go off with the men. Instead I was led to the German soldiers' barracks and offices. I was scared to death on that first morning that I was separated from the men. I thought that they knew that I'd lied about my age. I worried I'd be killed. Much to my relief I spent that day cleaning offices and shining boots. This is what I did every day. I can't tell you how many boots and shoes I shined: hundreds and hundreds for sure.

The German soldiers were all regular *Wehrmacht*, not those crazy SS men. These soldiers were actually pretty decent. Of course they had a job to do, so they couldn't get all buddy-buddy with you. However they weren't hell-bent on making you suffer either.

There were no barbed wire fences or towers at Jeleśnia. Those would all come later. We were surrounded by plenty of armed soldiers, and even though they weren't horrible, we knew they'd shoot us if we didn't do what we were told.

After a couple weeks, three or four, we got to know some of the guards (Actually the men did. I kept my mouth shut). One spoke a little Polish, and we'd learned a little German; so some of the men asked this guy, "What happened to the women, children, and elderly?"

As I've said I'd hoped that somehow I'd see my mother and siblings again, and even though I'd pretty much decided it wasn't going to happen, this was when I first heard for sure. The soldier told us they'd all been killed.

My father was a pretty tough man. If the news surprised him or upset him, he didn't show it. Maybe he already knew in his heart they were dead. Therefore what the soldier said didn't faze him. And like I've explained, he wasn't much of a talker, so it's not like we sat in his bunk and had a big father-son talk about it that night. The news made me extremely sad and incredibly angry. I thought about grabbing a soldier's rifle and killing every single German, but that was childish bravado, wishful nonsense. In reality I knew it would be fruitless suicide. My family had been murdered. There was nothing I could do.

Even though I believed my mother and siblings were dead, a little part of me kept thinking, "But maybe they're not. Maybe somehow they survived." I guess that's normal. But here's something interesting. Even as I'm telling you all this, some Red Cross records have been found that list a Hannah Urman still alive at Auschwitz in 1944! Some very sharp historians with the St. Louis Holocaust Museum are helping me look into this.

Maybe that little spark of doubt inside of me wasn't all that foolish. What if somehow my mother survived? Even if she had made it all the way to the very end, large numbers of survivors died during and after soon after liberation. We were all sick and starving, and the Germans were doing their best to do us in before the Allies arrived. And even if she somehow survived until liberation, many people died because they were too far gone. Nothing could help them. In spite of the great care we were given, still many, many died.

I still have a little pinch of hope. Call it hope or fantasy or whatever you like, but what's the harm in it? So what if I still have a little bit of that ten year-old boy in me who wonders if somehow she survived? Maybe she looked and looked for me, as I looked for her? Perhaps she gave up, just as I gave up and moved away to start a new life? I know this is all just wishful thinking, but forgive me. I've been through a little bit of trouble in life. I deserve a little wishful thinking.

I also have my own very, very strong doubts that she could have possibly still been alive as late as 1944. I just can't picture my mother, my pillar of strength, allowing her infant and two children to be taken from her. In my mind, my mother would have fought to keep them. She would have died trying. Then, do I betray my own memory of my beloved mother, when I allow myself to think she may have been alive in 1944?

A close friend has shared a thought that may allow me to live with my seemingly conflicted mind. He said, "Ben, maybe your mother knew that her baby and two children were doomed. In a split second she decided to live in the hopes that you would survive. Perhaps her great strength of character enabled her to mourn the loss of her other children, while driving herself to stay alive for years in the camps, simply hoping that she could one day see you, her only surviving son, sometime again?"

I like this thought, but to be honest the issue is not yet settled in my mind. That's okay. Having all of life's mysteries settled is a pipe dream for the young and the foolish. Some things we just can't figure out. Maybe there's an answer booth in Heaven where we can finally learn all these things.

Winter was gradually coming on. So, on top of not getting enough of even lousy food, life was complicated by the cold. The barracks had two pot-bellied stoves, and the Germans left small amounts of coal outside. My hard wooden bunk had only a straw mattress and a thin blanket, but with the stoves it was tolerable. Thankfully we spent most of our time indoors. Of course, we had to go outside to walk to and from work, as well as to stand in line for the morning and evening meals. Walking helped generate just enough heat to make it tolerable. Waiting in line for food did not. Even a slight breeze would blow the cold right through me. The bowl of hot soup at the end of the line, as terrible as it was, kept me going.

There were a couple of kitchens at the camp, and we had to stand outside in line for 30-45 minutes to get a little bowl of horrid soup and, maybe, a chunk of hard, black bread. We'd been given some clothes, but they weren't adequate. We had no gloves. This was Poland in the dead of winter, so being outside was no treat. But we were all Poles. We'd had more than our share of cold winters with little to eat. Even so, not everyone survived.

Time passed, and the winter wore on. Each day was just like the other. We worked, we slept, and we ate whatever was provided. I missed my family horribly. My father was there, but he offered no comfort. It's as if he was born with a complete lack of fatherly instincts. Did it ever cross his mind that although I was trying my best to be strong, to be brave, I was actually heartbroken and terrified? While he said very little and offered no encouragement, thankfully, several of the guys in the barracks did. I can't remember any of their names, but I owe them an enormous debt of gratitude. Without their occasional pats on the back and words of encouragement, I may have given up.

Eventually winter gave way to spring. One day they separated us by age and reassigned us to buildings and bunks. I can't remember my new barracks number, but I guess that doesn't matter. This is when I was separated from my father. I was alone, but that didn't make things any scarier. Like I said, my dad wasn't much of a husband or a father. I honestly didn't care where he went. I know this sounds bad, but it's the truth. Had he been there at all for me, even the tiniest bit, I would have done anything for him.

At this point they brought in kapos to watch over us. The SS had hand-picked especially brutal criminals from prisons to serve as kapos. They were rewarded for their work with more and better food, more sleep, and no physical labor. If a kapo was found to be too easy on the prisoners under his charge, the SS would demote him and move him back to normal prison life. This made them very motivated to make life a living hell for us. They were there to watch and listen to us and report any trouble makers or slackers to the Germans.

A couple days later we were called out of the buildings and made to line up at attention. Some of the older men were pulled aside and left on trucks. The Germans didn't tell us where they were going; but, I supposed they were being taken away to be murdered.

Next the Germans gave us each a little chunk of bread with a small bit of cheese and told us we were leaving Jeleśnia. I can't tell you for certain, but my best guess is that we'd stayed at Jeleśnia for about eight months. I didn't know where we were going.

It was spring, so it wasn't cold. The sky was a dull grey, but it didn't look like rain. Starting with those closest to the road, the Germans formed us into a column about four to five men abreast. Thus we marched out of camp and down the road. I believe they were emptying the whole camp, so there were thousands of us in the column. I couldn't tell you exactly how many because when you're in the middle of it all, you can only really see the area around you. But when we'd get to the top of a hill, I could see ahead and behind a little farther. Thousands, is my best guess.

I hadn't seen my father among those selected out and put into trucks, so I assumed he must be somewhere along the vast column. He could have been twenty feet or two hundred yards from me. Where he was didn't matter. I knew he could take care of himself. That's all he'd been doing his entire life. And I knew I could take care of myself. I'd been doing so since Bedzin. What choice did I have?

None of us knew where we were going, but that didn't stop the guys from asking one another. Guys would even ask me. I was just a kid; how in world would I have known more than my elders?

It wasn't a hard march. At this point the Germans weren't trying to kill us. They wanted us for labor, so the pace was reasonable. We stopped for a brief break every three hours or so. Trucks would come by with a little food and water once or twice a day. I don't believe any of the men were a day over thirty, so everyone was able to keep up. That wasn't the case during later marches.

The march would stop each night. We'd sleep on the ground huddled together to keep warm. I was exhausted from walking all day; so even though the ground was hard, and it was a little chilly, I slept. Each morning we'd wake before dawn to the blowing of shrill whistles and harsh shouts, "*Raus! Raus!*" I'd rub my aching muscles and stand up as quickly as possible. My clothes were damp from the early morning dew, which made me chilly and actually eager to get moving. Marching would warm me up and loosen up my sore muscles.

The march continued on without much happening for five, or maybe six, days. We were in the countryside, and every so often we'd pass a little farmhouse. I don't remember ever seeing anyone out and about at the farms. Maybe the houses had been occupied by Jews who'd already been taken away. Maybe they weren't Jews, but they thought it would be best to stay inside while the long line of prisoners marched by.

Finally we reached Blechhammer. It was a real camp. It was the beginning of the barbed wires, and striped clothing, and my number. At Blechhammer the Germans gave me a new name. They even tattooed it on my arm, I guess so I'd never forget it. My new name was 178873. Forget Ben Fainer or anything like that.

Chapter Six

Blechhammer

There wasn't much to the entrance of Blechhammer. We entered through a tall, simple gate hung from a sturdy, wooden frame. A formidable barbed wire fence strung off from each side of the gate and surrounded the camp. Next to the gate was a two-story, concrete guard house. The first story had two small rectangle openings. These were gun holes. The second story had open sides and a wooden roof. Guards with machine guns stood in the tower looking down at us as we passed by. It was quite intimidating.

A friend of mine recently showed me a photo of this very guard tower, which stands to this day. You could have knocked me over with a feather. I haven't watched any of the Holocaust movies. I've tried my best to avoid viewing photos. Before showing me the photo, he assured me the photo didn't show any of the horror. It was just a photo of how the gate looks today. Seeing the photo made my heart race; the memories came flooding back. I said to him, "Do you believe that I was there? That I saw this with my own eyes?" He, of course, said that he did. "I don't! I see this, but I still can't believe this was real. I can't believe I went through all this."

Then he showed me a map of Blechhammer. I couldn't believe there was so much more to it than I'd ever imagined. However, you must understand; I only saw what was right in front of me. I'd trained myself not too look around. Looking around brought attention to yourself. Believe me you don't want attention. You learn to blend in. Therefore, looking at the map, I was surprised by the camp's size. But of course, I was there early on, so they may have added quite a bit later on. The parts that I remember were all there on the map: the gate, the barracks, and the SS section. It all came flowing back. I remember it all in such vivid detail. If telling my story wasn't so important, I'd pray day and night for Almighty God to erase each and every memory.

We entered the camp and were marched down a road that was just wide enough for two trucks to fit through. To our left, which was the center of the camp, was the SS section. It was surrounded by a tall barbed wire fence and held the SS offices and barracks. Along the other side of the road, we passed a series of long, low barracks.

I think there were about 30 to 40 wooden barracks at Blechhammer. Unlike the forced labor camp at Jelesnia, the camp was surrounded by barbed wire fences, with guard towers, like the one near the gate, placed evenly along the walls.

Even though the camp looked quite imposing, Blechhammer wasn't so bad in the beginning. At first we were guarded by the *Wehrmacht*. These were regular army soldiers who'd been trained for war. They were actually fairly nice. But there was about one SS soldier for every ten *Wehrmacht*. Therefore they couldn't be too nice. They had a job to do and didn't want to get killed by the SS any more than we did.

So all and all, things weren't too bad in the beginning. They shaved me from head-to-toe and took away my normal clothes. From then on I only wore clothing that looked like striped pajamas. We slept two to a bunk and were given an extra pair of pants and a shirt. We were usually given two meals a day. The food was horrible, but compared to what we'd get later it wasn't all that bad.

There was an ongoing debate among the guys about eating all your bread right away, versus saving a little to eat later. This was the subject of many of our discussions before drifting off to sleep in our bunks. One side would argue that every bit of food should always be eaten right away. For one thing, they'd say, you never know what might happen. A kapo could knock you down and your saved bread might fall out. Also, they argued, you should get all the nutrients inside and helping you as soon as you can.

The other side held that it would better help you to get through your day if you had a little bread saved for later. This would give you something to look forward to and would give you a little burst of energy to keep you going.

I didn't say much during these arguments. I wasn't used to speaking among adults, especially among men. I usually saved a little bread for later, but sometimes I'd eat the whole thing. I wasn't a strict member of either side of the debate. Some guys were and got really intense about it during the discussions. I just did whatever I felt like at the time. Either way we were starving. We never got much, and what little we got never filled you up.

Every morning before dawn they'd roust us from our bunks and make us stand for roll call along the road that separated our barracks from the SS part of the camp. Most times the count would go by pretty quickly, thus we only had to stand at attention for 30-45 minutes. Other times, I guess if the kapos or guards had messed up on the count, roll call could go on for an hour or two.

Standing at roll call probably seems simple enough. You might think; at least we weren't marching or being made to work for hours on end. However it was actually one of the scariest and most physically demanding times of the day. As I've mentioned, blending in is one of the most important survival skills in the camps. When marching everyone is all spread along the road, and the guards and kapos are also marching. With everyone in motion, it's very easy to go along unnoticed. Work was the same way, with everyone doing his own job and the kapos moving from place to place, it was fairly easy to blend in. You developed a sixth sense of knowing when a kapo was approaching, so you could pick up the pace a little.

But there was no place to hide during roll call. Everyone was evenly spread out in rows and columns across the roll call yard. Everything was in precise geometric form. The SS men and kapos could scan the yard and easily spot any sign of disorder. Even the slightest disturbance quickly drew attention. Is someone too weak or sick to stand without swaying or stumbling? This must be investigated. This prisoner may be too weak to work. And if he's too weak to work, he's of no use to the Third Reich.

I would stand there and hope to God the count would go well. I'd hear the footsteps of an SS guard coming down the row behind me. I'd tell myself to stand straight and to be still. I'd want to look to see if he was heading for me, but I'd will myself to remain calm and to keep my eyes cast down at the ground just before my feet.

Then I'd be swept over by a great wave of relief as he passed on by. Yes, he might stop and test another prisoner's fitness to work. And yes, that prisoner might end up taken away to be killed. And that, of course, was a tragedy. But it wasn't me. It wasn't me during that roll call, on that morning, of that day. You see we didn't live week-by-week or day-by-day in the camps. We lived minute-by-minute.

When morning roll call was finally completed the men were marched out through the front gate. As one long column they made a right on the road outside the camp and headed to work in nearby fac-tories. It would take 30-40 minutes for all the men to march out of camp.

Since I was the youngest, they didn't make me march to work. Instead, after the last of the men marched out the front gate, they'd walk me and a few other young guys to the SS section of the camp. The gate into this area was just inside the camp opposite the front gate. All day long I'd go from building-to-building and from room-to-room. I'd clean their barracks and the offices and shine their shoes. Later in the evening we'd be led back out of the SS section and watch as the men would return to the camp. This is what happened every day.

One morning at roll call a *Wehrmacht* guard stopped in front of me and asked, "Why are your shoes not shined?" I was wearing the shoes we'd been issued, which had wooden soles, a toe section of black leather, and a foot section of canvas. They laced up the front and were about ankle-high. I guess since I shined a lot of SS boots every day, this guard thought my own should look better. Maybe he was just looking to give me a hard time. There may not have been any good way to answer his question, but I know for sure that I made the worst possible decision in opening my big mouth. I don't know what in the world came over me. How could I have been so stupid! I said in a matter of fact tone, "I didn't feel like shining them."

He took a step back, swung the butt of his rifle up, and struck me on the jaw below the left side of my chin. The force knocked me down and split open my chin. My vision blurred and my head spun. I was afraid I might pass out and fall to the ground. That could have been the end of me. I shouted to myself inside my head, "Stand up! Stand up!" Though darkness was starting to close in from the edges of my vision, I somehow managed to get back to my feet. I kept my head turned down and dared not look up at the guard. I counted two or three heartbeats and braced myself for another blow.

Through my clouded vision, I could just make out his boots before me, which much to my relief spun around and walked away. I kept my eyes cast downward, holding my breath, hoping he wouldn't come back. My chin hurt like hell, and as my vision gradually cleared, I could see a large red stain spreading down my striped shirt from the blood flowing out of a deep gash. That was a very long and frightening day of work. While I gradually started feeling better by midday, I was terribly worried that the gash and blood would draw attention. I was afraid my blood might drip on the SS office floors or onto their boots. Thankfully, if any of the SS men even noticed my condition, none seemed to care.

I'd been dangerously stupid. He could have just as easily shot me in the head or crushed my skull. I caught hell from my bunk mates later that night. I didn't mind though. They were just looking after me. Since I was so young and all alone, a lot of the guys went out of their way to watch over me. I was lucky to have survived my utter stupidity. I was even luckier the cut did not get infected. It actually healed pretty well considering the filth we lived in. I carry the scar to this day as a reminder that it never pays to be a wise guy.

Over the next several months the *Wehrmacht* were gradually replaced by SS soldiers. This changed the tone of the camp quite a bit. More lookout towers were added, each bristling with more machine guns. They ordered the construction of gallows along both sides of the fence just inside the front gate. Discipline also changed; the SS were more aggressive and less tolerant of prisoners who struggled to keep up. Without a doubt, had I mouthed off to one of the SS monsters, I would not have lived to tell this tale. I would have been beaten to death on the spot or ended up dangling by my neck from the newly erected gallows.

The kapos spied on us, so you had to watch what you said around them. If you were sick, you had to try and act fine around them. If you weren't working hard enough, or if they caught you stealing food, they'd turn you in. Then, as everyone was returning through the gates in the evening, we'd see people the kapos turned in hanging by their necks from gallows. The Germans didn't place hoods over their heads. Their bulging eyes stared out at us. They'd leave the bodies hanging there for days just to teach everyone a lesson. This is what I had to look at every day. It was horrific. It still haunts me, ever more so since I've broken my silence. I'm right back there in my nightmares. Their eyes stare down at me accusingly, "Why did you make it? Why did I end this way?" I wake in a cold sweat, trembling, and muttering, "I don't know. I just don't know."

At first when I saw a horrible act of cruelty, such as a kapo beating a man for working too slowly, I'd turn my head. I didn't want to see it. Out of respect for the person being beaten, I didn't want him to see me watching. At the time I thought that somehow I was helping the poor man retain a small bit of his dignity. Now I realize that this was simply my own way of trying to hold onto my own humanity, my own dignity. Whether I looked or turned away was most likely of no concern to a man being brutally attacked. He was only concerned with surviving the torment and pleading with Almighty God.

After a while you didn't bother turning away. You still see it happening, but somehow it just doesn't register. And why waste the energy turning away? You're just as likely to see something worse looking elsewhere. This sounds harsh, but maybe your heart has to harden in order to survive. Thankfully this hardening wasn't permanent. I'm a strong man, but I have a very soft heart. It's my nature. The Nazis took everything else dear to me, but at least I have that.

I was the youngest, and I was alone. I didn't know where my father was, and like I said, I didn't really care. I simply focused on staying alive by working hard and keeping my mouth shut. But I wasn't really alone.

Let's put it this way, the camaraderie among the guys was indescribable! As I mentioned, since I was so young a lot of the guys kept an eye on me and encouraged me. So when I used to clean up the SS offices and barracks, if someone had left a half-eaten sandwich lying around or in the trash can, I would smuggle it under my clothes to bring back for the guys.

If the SS men weren't around or weren't looking, I would steal one of their cigarettes from a pack on a desk. I'd hide the cigarette between my butt cheeks and bring it back for the guys.

Most prisoners never smoked cigarettes. Instead they would trade them to kapos in exchange for extra soup or bread. Whenever you saw a regular prisoner smoking a cigarette, you knew he'd given up. To someone like that a cigarette was a final luxury before death.

The SS officers at this point didn't go out of their way to be cruel. Don't get me wrong; these were trained killers. They were never nice. But for the most part, as long as you could work, they left you alone. While I was working they didn't say much, just things like, "Make it quick, Jew!"

We'd finish one room and move onto the next. We were rarely left alone, so I had to be very quick and very careful stealing scraps of food or cigarettes to bring back for the guys. The best time to steal was near the very end of the work day. First of all, there were more food scraps after the SS men had lunch. Secondly, I didn't want to risk walking around all day hiding food scraps in my clothes or a cigarette in between my butt cheeks.

Obviously I never got caught because I'm alive telling you all this. Had I gotten caught, I would have joined the poor guys hanging from ropes by the gates. But I had to take the risk for the guys because they were so good to me. They helped me so much and always encouraged me, saying things like, "Ben, you got to stay alive. You always got to be pumped up."

One evening, after we'd returned from our day's work and eaten our small bit of food, the Germans made us form a very long single file line. I was somewhere in the middle of the line, which at its front led into a barracks. As usual all the guys in line kept asking the same type of questions they'd always ask, "What is this? What is going to happen?" And, as always, none of us knew.

After about four or five hours, I finally reached the entrance to the barracks. I stepped inside and saw about a dozen tables spread out across the otherwise empty barracks. One or two SS men stood beside each table, one of whom was holding some type of metal instrument I'd never seen before. Immediately I was sent to stand by a table off to the left side of the room. There was only one SS man there, and he was holding the strange instrument.

He was probably about 25 or 30 years old, but I don't really remember exactly what he looked like, other than that I can say he looked like a mean son-of-a-bitch, if you'll pardon my French. With a cigarette dangling from his lips, he asked my name, which he wrote in a ledger. He grabbed my wrist and squeezed my arm very tightly. Using the metal instrument, he began tattooing the number 178873 across the top side of my left forearm.

It hurt like hell as the tattoo needle at the end of the instrument poked down again and again about ¼ of an inch into my skin. I didn't scream or cry. None of the guys did. I probably groaned a little. When the SS man was finished, he wiped the blood away with a filthy rag and double checked the tattoo with the number in his ledger. With a grunt, he pointed to the door. I was now 178873 – forget Ben. He was gone.

I returned to my barracks and went right to sleep. It was very late. I'd worked all day, stood in line for four or five hours and then finally gotten a number tattooed into my arm. Why not go to sleep? Why stay up and ask the guys a bunch of questions about this strange new development? None of us knew anything.

The tattooing continued in the same way for two or three more nights until everyone in the camp had a number. I've learned an interesting thing about my number, 178873. I read somewhere the first 3,056 male prisoners of Blechhammer were given tattoos of the Auschwitz-numbers 176,512 through 179,567. Blechhammer was technically a part of the expansive Auschwitz system of camps, sub-camps, and dozens and dozens of small force-labor camps. The number on my arm has caused a bit of confusion.

There are several Red Cross documents listing me as having been a prisoner at Auschwitz. I was in the Auschwitz system. I was never in the main camp of Auschwitz, the one that people visit and see in all the movies.

At the end of most days, usually about 8:30 or 9:30 in the evening, the men would return from working in the factories. We'd wait in line for a little soup and chunk of hard bread, and then we'd head to our bunks back in the barracks. By 11:00 we'd collapse into sleep.

A lot of nights we'd do a little bit of chatting in the barracks before going to sleep. Sometimes we'd talk about our favorite meals from back home and what we'd eat if we ever got out of this God forsaken place. That kind of talk would only make us hungrier, but it never stopped us from talking about it. Guys would describe a favorite meal in excruciating detail. I could close my eyes and see it very clearly in my mind. I couldn't smell or taste it, which was extremely frustrating. But I could see it, and that was something.

I never said much during these discussions because I was the youngest. I did, however, tell them about my mother's goulash. This started a quiet, but heated, argument over whose mother made the best goulash. They were older, and I kept pretty quiet, so I'm sure the guys felt confident that they won the argument. But I knew the truth. My beloved mother made the best goulash in the entire world. No question about it.

Mostly they asked each other the same stupid questions they always asked each other, "What's going to happen to us?" "What will happen tomorrow?" Sometimes I'd finally have enough of these endless questions, and even though they were older, I'd say, "Shut up! Enough of this. Stop worrying all the time. Be strong!"

If we weren't exhausted, it would have been utterly impossible to sleep in those conditions. They never replaced the straw mattresses, which after a short time were flat, filthy, and crawling with lice and other insects. We were crowded, crammed into row after row of shelf-like bunks, sleeping three or four to a bunk. The bunks were a little longer than normal beds, so there was just enough room for four. Since there was little heat in the barracks, sleeping crowded among two or three other bodies helped to keep us from freezing. And, of course, there was quite a bit of snoring.

So no way you'd get any sleep if you were just a normal person, under normal circumstances. But we were no longer normal people. It had been a very long time since we'd lived under normal circumstances. I was 9 ½ years old when I entered the forced labor camp at Jeleśnia. By the time I left Blechhammer I was about 11 ½ years old.

More or less the day I've just described to you was repeated everyday for the 14 to 15 months I was kept at Blechhammer. Then one morning the siren went off in the morning, and as usual we formed our lines out in the yard. Without fanfare an SS officer announced, "We're leaving here."

Just as we'd marched out of Jeleśnia, we formed a long column of about four to five men abreast and walked out the gate at Blechhammer. I remember that there was no "Work will set you free" sign above the gate at Blechhammer. The sign simply read, "Blechhammer."

As usual all the guys around me started whispering to each other, "Where are we going?" "What's going to happen?" I looked at the sky. It was cloudy, but it didn't look like rain. The temperature was mild, maybe about 45 degrees. I told myself, "Don't worry. Keep strong." And I marched.

I'm sure I looked very different from the time I'd entered Blechhammer to the time I'd left it. Of course there were no mirrors in the camp, but I knew what the other guys looked like. Also there were no watches, nor calendars. We never knew the day of the week and only guessed the months by the change of the season. When I tell you I was in the forced labor camp at Jeleśnia for about 7 or 8 months, it's only my best guess. It could have been a little more. It could have been a little less. The same is true for my time at Blechhammer. I think I was there for about 14 to 16 months. It could have been a little more or a little less. The exact time doesn't really matter. The important thing is that I was there, and I had survived. Many, many people hadn't.

Chapter Seven

Into Germany

The march out of Blechhammer to our unknown destination lasted about 5 ½ days. What can I tell you? It was very much like the march from Jeleśnia to Blechhammer. Each day we woke just before dawn and ate a little bit of soup and bread. The soup was not like any soup you've ever had. It was stuff left over from the guards' kitchens, such as potato peelings, boiled for a while in water. The bread was hard and usually black. I've read that sawdust was often mixed in so the Germans could conserve their wheat.

We marched all day and into the night stopping occasionally for a break. At night we ate again and slept. It wasn't so bad especially compared to later marches. At this point we were still useful to the Germans. They needed us alive and relatively healthy so we could work.

The second day of the march was a little tougher as it rained all day. Thankfully it stopped before we slept. The third day was dry, but on the fourth day it rained again. This time it rained all night, so we slept very little. As we were huddled together in the rain on the fourth night, some of the guys mentioned that we'd passed into Germany earlier in the evening. They'd noticed the signs in a little village we passed through were all in German. This was news to me.

When I was marching, hour after hour, day after day, all I thought about was, "keep walking." I had barely noticed a little village, let alone seeing signs in German.

You'd think I would have been flabbergasted finding out I'd left my homeland and entered Germany. I mean, for the first 9 ½ years of my life, I'd never been more than a mile or so from my home. But to be honest it didn't faze me one bit. Maybe I was too exhausted. I don't know.

At least now our usual conversation had a little twist to it that night in the rain. Instead of saying, "Where are we going?" "What's going to happen?" the guys could add, "My God, we're in Germany; where are we going?" or "Now that we're in Germany, what's going to happen?" And of course the Germans never told us a thing, so what did we know?

As the rainy night drew on, even though we were all huddled together, I became very cold and started to shiver uncontrollably. I allowed myself to think about coming in from the freezing cold after fetching the water back in Bedzin. I imagined my dear mother wrapping me in her arms, losing myself in her warm embrace, as we stood together next to the tile oven in the kitchen. With those painfully wonderful thoughts in mind, I must have drifted off to sleep for a bit.

On the fifth day I woke to find that it had stopped raining sometime in the early morning. It was cloudy, but it looked as if the rain was finished. Whenever we marched they must have taken us on routes plotted to avoid cities and villages as best they could. We passed some farm houses and tiny villages that day. In Poland people stayed inside while our long column marched past. However in Germany some of the people stood outside and watched. They didn't say anything, but they watched.

About mid-day we approached a large camp surrounded by tall barbed wire fences. Guard towers with machine guns were spaced at even intervals along the fence. As my section of the long column of men approached the entrance, I saw a sign with the name "Buchenwald." Beyond there were rows and rows of barracks as far as the eye could see.

Now I should tell you a little bit I've learned about these camps. You should understand that I didn't know any of this back then. My view of things was limited to only a little bit of all that was going on. I only knew about what was right in front of me. We had no access to radios or newspapers, and the Germans never told us a thing.

Unlike the camps in Poland, which the Germans could not begin constructing until after their invasion in September of 1939, the camps in Germany had been in the works since Hitler first came to power. The first was Dachau, which opened on March 22, 1933, just 51 days after Hitler took power. "Work will set you free" was on a sign at Dachau's gate.

Buchenwald was constructed in 1937. The camp was not designnated as an extermination camp, but I've read that as many as 56,000 people died there. They died from starvation, being worked to death, disease, and execution. The sign at Buchenwald's gate did not have the work slogan, but rather, "*Jedem das Seine*," which basically means "everyone gets what he deserves." With that in mind, I believe the sign was wrong in 55,999 of the deaths.

You see, the second commandant, Karl Otto Kock, ran the camp from 1937 to 1941. He may have been there while I was there, I don't know; it's not like the big shots went door-to-door welcoming you to their camp. But anyway, his wife was known as "*Die Hexe von Buchenwald*," which means, "the witch of Buchenwald" because she was horribly cruel. I remember hearing a little bit about her; you know when guys would talk a little bit in the barracks. They didn't call her the "Witch of Buchenwald" though. They called her the "Bitch of Buchenwald." God knows what she did to earn that title in a place where horror and brutality were as common as flies over dead bodies.

Koch eventually ended up a prisoner of Buchenwald himself for corruption, embezzlement, and other bureaucratic misbehavior. He was executed by firing squad on April 5, 1945, a short while before the Americans liberated the camp. So the sign was indeed accurate for Commandant Koch; he got what he deserved. His wife also was charged and held in the camp, but was eventually released. She was later arrested and sentenced to life in prison. In September of 1967 she committed suicide while in a Bavarian prison.

The Germans executed Soviet prisoners of war at Buchenwald. Over 1,000 were shot in the back of the head in 1941 and 1942. After the war the Soviet Union used the camp for about five years as a prison for Nazis. From what I've heard, the Soviets could be quite cruel.

I dearly hope they kept the "everyone gets what he deserves" sign hanging at the gate.

It was late afternoon by the time I marched through the gate at Buchenwald. I saw a sign that said, "Buchenwald." But I don't remember seeing the "everyone gets what he deserves" sign. To be honest it could have been right there, but I just didn't notice. The gate was built into a large three story building. The other day I looked at an old photograph of the gate and noticed it had a clock tower on its roof. I don't remember ever seeing this clock, but it may have been there. Honestly it was simply too dangerous to walk around looking at things, and a clock was absolutely of no use.

The barbed wire fences seemed higher than at Blechhammer, and the tall wooden guard towers, manned by soldiers holding machine guns, seemed more numerous as well.

There might have been a large metal eagle on an archway over the top of the gate, but that may have been at Dachau, which comes later. I marched into a lot of different camps. It's easy to get the gates a little mixed up. I was focused on surviving. That's really all I thought about. Marching for 5 ½ days in all kinds of weather wasn't like a walk in the park. You didn't stop to admire the scenery or the decor of a camp gate. You might risk a quick glance when you arrive at a new camp, but nothing more.

We were led to an enormous yard. It was many, many times larger than the road that served as our yard at Blechhammer. While the Germans went through the lengthy process of assigning us to barracks, which were called blocks at Buchenwald, we were made to stand at attention spaced out in precise rows across yard. Eventually I was assigned to Block 15 along with 300 to 400 other guys.

As we walked a little ways to Block 15, I noticed there were a lot more barracks compared to Blechhammer. They were similar to those at Blechhammer, but packed together a little more tightly.

I saw there were two unusual open-aired sheds, with tall smoke stacks, directly next to Block 15. As we arrived there was no smoke coming from the stacks. The buildings were both quiet, that is, I didn't see anyone coming or going from them.

I was assigned a top bunk with two other guys. We rested in our bunks until later that evening, when we were called outside to get a bowl of rotten garbage boiled in water for dinner. The food at Jeleśnia and Blechhammer was bad enough, but it was utterly horrifying at Buchenwald.

After eating we returned to our bunks. We chatted a little about home towns, jobs, and family last names. A guy asked, "Has anyone seen my father, Abraham Rosenberg? We were separated during the march." No one had. I don't remember if this was the actual name; I'm simply using it as an example. I heard the same type of question asked over and over again in the camps. Rarely someone did indeed have a bit of knowledge about the person in question. In these cases good news about the person was rarer still. I never bothered asking if anyone had seen my father. I knew how to get by well enough on my own.

Chapter Eight

A Man

We were rousted from our bunks prior to dawn the next morning.
As we shuffled outside, I saw there was still no smoke coming from
the chimneys. I didn't see anyone around them either. We made our
way to the yard for roll call. The yard at Buchenwald was enormous.
If I remember correctly, there were actually two large, identical yards
situated just inside the front gate. As far as I could tell the entire camp
assembled there: thousands and thousands of us. The guards were still
mostly *Wehrmacht*, regular German army soldiers.

We stood waiting for about 45 minutes as the Germans counted us
and eventually started breaking us into work groups. Block 15 was
combined with a number of nearby blocks into a work detail of about
1,000 men. After a time our group started marching toward the gate.
For the first time I had not been separated out from the men. I marched with them out the front gate. I didn't know where we were going
or what type of work we'd be doing. However this did not worry me.
Rather I felt a little sense of pride that day. In Judaism a young male
becomes a man at age 13. The event is marked by a very special ceremony called a Bar Mitzvah. I was not yet 13, but on that morning in
Buchenwald I became a man.

48

This was a great relief to me. I'd always feared being separated out from the men. I had felt quite vulnerable. It made me stand out, and I worried that it made me appear less useful than a grown man. Marching among the throng of a thousand or so men made me feel nearly invisible. This seemed to be a much safer situation than being separated out as too young. I felt about as safe as anyone could, considering I was being starved and held prisoner by an army of ruthless murderers.

We marched for about three or four miles passing many factories the Germans had constructed around the camp. The factories, using tens of thousands of forced laborers, produced a wide variety of items needed to supply the German war effort. They divided up the jobs so that you never really knew what was being produced. Each group of workers only saw their own little part of the process. I guess they figured if we knew we were producing airplane parts or whatever, we might try to sabotage them. But if we didn't know what was being made, we'd just do our job.

Our group came to an enormous brick and stone factory. I estimate it was probably as long as a runway at a major airport. Giant smoke stacks rose up here and there across the vast facility. We'd passed numerous similar factories on our way to our factory, each filled with other slave laborers from the camp.

I was assigned to load boxes coming into one end of the factory onto a cart. Once loaded I would push the cart quite a ways across the factory to another door. There I would unload the boxes and return to get more. That's what I did all day, every day. I never saw what was in the boxes. I never saw what was done with them on the other side of the door where I delivered them. They could have been filled with ammunition or cans of beef stew; I didn't know, and I didn't care. All I cared about was doing my job, not being noticed, and not getting injured.

After a while we took a little break and went outside where trucks had pulled up with more horrible food. We stood in line, received a bowl of soup, ate, and returned to work.

Late in the evening we finished up for the day and marched back to camp. I rested for a while in my bunk until the siren sounded for our evening meal. Again I noted that nothing was going on at the two sheds with chimneys that stood no more than about eight to ten feet from the end of Block 15.

That night I asked the guys in the bunk about the buildings. Remember, I was the youngest, I didn't know anything. I'd never seen buildings like these. The guys told me they were crematoriums: ovens used to burn dead bodies. With that on my mind I drifted off to sleep. This is how I ended my first day as a man.

Chapter Nine

Smoke from the Chimneys

Within a week to ten days of our arrival at Buchenwald, the *Wehrmach* were replaced by SS men. The SS men were monsters. They lived to weed out the weak and wear down the strong.

I think this was late summer or early fall in 1941. Many years later I read the Nazi leaders met on January 20, 1942, at Wannsee, a suburb of Berlin, to plot out the best way to move forward in killing off all the Jews. The resulting plan was called the Final Solution, and it included marching thousands of Jews from camps in the east (Poland) to forced labor camps in the west (Germany).

They predicted that many of the weak would die along the way. They, of course, believed this to be a good outcome. Oddly though, they were concerned that the survivors would be made up of only the strongest and hardiest prisoners. This worried them as they thought we might be more likely to rebel. I think there is something perversely funny about their fear. Here they were trying to kill us off, so they could build their "master race." Then, by applying their own idiotic "survival of the fittest" theories to us, they fretted they might accidently create a group of super-prisoners! Hogwash! Utter hogwash! I didn't survive because I was stronger or smarter than any of the poor

51

souls who didn't. I survived. They didn't. It could have easily been the reverse. That's all there is to it.

Part of the Final Solution was what they called *Vernichtung durch Arbeit*, which means, "Extermination through Labor." This is a fancy way of saying, "working people to death." The Germans had two seemingly opposing goals relative to the Jews and the other undesirables. They needed us as slave labor to support their massive war effort. On the other hand, they wanted to exterminate us.

On such a massive scale it's surprisingly very difficult to exterminate people. As the war wore on, the Germans became more and more efficient at this horrendous task. Very early on they tried execution by gunfire. This took too much time and used up too many bullets that were needed for the war. Next they tried small trucks specially fitted to fill the cargo area with the truck's exhaust. They also tried piping truck exhaust into small rooms. These methods also took too much time and used too many precious resources. So eventually they settled on building massive gas chambers, such as those at Birkenau (the death camp at Auschwitz), in which the very young, very old, and the sick were exterminated. This, paired with working people to death, became their most efficient methods. It also provided a kind of balance between their goals of forced labor and extermination.

Dealing with so many bodies became a major problem. Initially they tried mass burials, but they soon ran out of space around the camps. Thus they built and used crematorium facilities, such as the one right outside Block 15. Even though they continued to upgrade these facilities, they simply could not keep up. Like I said, it's a very difficult task to murder millions, upon millions of people.

It makes me wonder how the war might have turned out differently for the Axis powers had they not been hell-bent on killing off millions of their citizens. These people, many among the most educated and productive within their societies, surely would have greatly benefited their economies and war effort. What if the enormous amounts of resources dedicated to enslaving and killing people had been focused instead on the war? Or even better yet, what if Hitler, instead of invading other nations, had focused all Germany's people on peacefully minding Germany's own business?

There have been cases of prisoners rising up here and there, but that was not an option at Buchenwald. We were a bunch of starving, exhausted men. How could we rebel against the SS monsters? We had nothing. They had guns, electrified barbed wire, and guard towers with machine guns. There was no way to escape. At night the entire camp was so well lit up by lights and search lights that you could have easily found a lost needle on the ground at midnight.

Every two to three days the Germans would make us switch bunks, mixing everyone up, so you never shared the same bunk with the same guys for long. I think they did this to keep us from working together, so we wouldn't organize some type of escape or resistance. If that was their reason, they really didn't need to go to all the trouble. We were too exhausted and weak to do anything other than merely survive.

They also switched our guards on a regular basis; I suppose to keep them from getting too familiar with any one group of prisoners. This too was probably unnecessary. The SS were brain-washed monsters. They believed we were sub-humans: pests that needed to be exterminated. Whether they became too familiar with us or not, none would have lifted a finger to help us.

Once or twice a month, after our evening meal, the SS would rush into the barracks armed with machine guns, yelling "Everybody out!" Exhausted from the day's work, we'd rise from our bunks and stand outside while they checked the barracks. They were looking for anything the guys may have picked up while away from the camp at work. I never took anything while at work. The risk was too great, and there was nothing I ever saw that I needed.

Everyone was starving. Everyone was exhausted. Diseases swept the camp. It got so I could spot a person who'd given up and know he'd be dead within a day or two.

A guy would be doing okay. Day-after-day he plodded along doing everything he could to survive. Then, for whatever reason, there'd be a changed look in his eyes, and I'd know right away he'd given up. Sometimes it was caused by sickness or starvation. When that was the case, I could see a change in the color of the face.

When it was just the change in the eyes, it wasn't so much a physical thing. I think for whatever reason the guy just gave up: lost his will-power to survive. I strongly believe the key to staying alive was learning to focus on staying alive that very moment. The guys who couldn't do this, the ones who got all caught up in worrying about days, weeks, months, and years of unknown horrors to come, were the ones who gave up. They simply became overwhelmed. There is a

Yiddish saying, "A broken spirit is hard to heal." In the camps a broken spirit never healed.

On several occasions I witnessed suicide. I heard of men who killed themselves by running into the electrified barbed wire fences, but I don't recall ever seeing this. If a prisoner simply walked into the space between the camp and the fence, he'd quickly get shot by the guards in the towers. He'd be dead long before he ever got close to the fence. This is how I saw men commit suicide. A few steps toward the fence were all that was needed.

I honestly never considered ending my life. I was taken away as a kid. I wanted to live a real life. I knew there was a big world out there: bigger than my home town, bigger than life in a filthy barracks. I wanted more than anything to get out there and see it. This was a very strong desire in my heart. It kept me going.

Focus on today. Focus on the very moment. Do that every moment. Do that every day, day-after-day. This was how I survived in the camps. This is how I've thrived ever since.

Some guys, especially those who were only a little older than I, had a little more pep in their spirits than the older guys. These guys encouraged me quite a bit. They'd say, "How are you doing? Don't give up. Maybe someday we'll get out of here. Are you going to make it?"

That would help me quite a bit. It would help to pump me up, so I could keep going. I'd answer, "Yes! I'm going to make it. How about you? Are you okay?"

At the end of every day we collapsed into our bunks. Of course there was the usual round of questions: one hundred variations of "What's going to happen next?" But we also asked each other where we were from and things like that. We were all Jews from Poland. Some of the guys were from my home town of Bedzin, others from nearby towns, still others from places I'd never heard of. Everyone spoke Yiddish.

I didn't recognize any of the guys from Bedzin. I really only knew the kids in my regular school and Hebrew school and, of course, my relatives. Also, we'd all been through quite a lot already, so even if one of the guys in Block 15 had lived right in my apartment building back in Bedzin, we probably wouldn't have recognized each other. Like I've said, we didn't have any mirrors, but I could see everyone else. I knew I looked the same.

The Nazi leaders may not have worked out the details of their Final Solution until January 1942, but I know firsthand that they were working us to death in 1941. The march to and from work became a living hell. With so little food and so little sleep (two or three hours a night), many, many people couldn't keep up. If a guy got dizzy and couldn't keep up, he'd get his face smashed by the butt of an SS rifle, or maybe shot in the head. Other guys collapsed and were just left to die along the side of the road. Day and night this went on. Day-after-day the bodies built up along the roadside. Birds flocked to the area and feasted on the fallen bodies. You couldn't take three or four steps during the three or four mile march without seeing another body.

Again I apologize for telling you such terrible things. I don't want to hold back, though. It's important for you to understand just how evil we humans can be. Otherwise it's too easy to think this could never happen again.

Every so often there'd be fewer bodies along the road. I guess the Germans forced a work detail to take them away while we were working at the factory. I don't know what they did with them; maybe they were buried in mass graves. I don't believe they were hauled all the way to the furnaces outside Block 15.

The marches to and from work were hell, but at this point being at Block 15 was even worse. Twenty-four hours a day, seven days a week, bodies piled up all around the crematorium sheds. Two man teams worked day and night under close SS supervision. They would place each body on a stretcher, carry it to the oven, open the furnace gate and slide the body in. I've read the crematorium workers were rewarded with adequate food and sleep for performing this horrific task.

The dead were brought in on large push carts and stacked in orderly piles. The crematorium buildings were open to the outdoors, so the furnaces were clearly visible from the area between them and our block. Conditions in Buchenwald were unbelievably harsh; people were dying faster than the Germans could burn them. The bodies stacked up outside the crematorium buildings rotting in the open air. The smell was unbearable.

They didn't just bring dead people to the crematorium buildings. They also brought many people who were very much alive, but too weak to work. So every time I walked out to go to work, every time I returned from work, I heard the screams from those who were still living. They moaned and cried from within the stacks of dead and live bodies. They screamed as they were slid on the metal carts through the open doors into the fiery furnaces.

I wished that I could have helped them, but there was nothing I could do. It kills me that I couldn't help. Every day I saw this. Every night I'd stand in line for 45 minutes waiting to get my bowl of soup to eat. I'd stand there seeing all this, hearing all this, smelling all this, while waiting to eat food that was a nightmare on its own. The ashes floated down upon us from the ceaseless smoke. The entire area around Block 15 was covered by a thick coat of ash. Twenty-four hours a day, seven days a week, the furnaces burned. Have you ever smelled burning flesh? There is no worse smell on earth. We breathed in the ashes of the dead with every breath. It was everywhere, even falling into what little food we ate. Can you imagine?

To tell you the truth, I can't believe it. I can't believe that I lived like that. I don't know how I survived. I don't know why I survived, while all those poor, poor people died in such a horrible way, in such a horrible place.

I've met one of the wonderful American soldiers who liberated Dachau. He said he could smell the camp from miles away, long before he could see it. He described it as an unholy smell. The smell at Block 15 was worse than unholy. Human waste fouled the very ground outside the barracks. There was a crude outhouse facility right near Block 15. It had four walls around a deep pit, a plank with four to five holes across the pit, and no roof. This crude facility was shared by a thousand guys. If the line was too long, some guys couldn't wait, especially if they were sick from Typhus or whatever. They'd squat wherever they could and relieve themselves right on the ground. Mixed with the smell of rotting corpses, and the smell of burning flesh, I can't believe that the bowels of Hell could smell any worse.

The SS were inhumane monsters. I will never forget the first time I saw one bayonet a guy at roll call for no apparent reason. The SS man was walking down the line and stopped in front of some poor guy and yelled, "What are you looking at? How dare you look at me!" The guy didn't answer, which was the safest thing to do. So the SS man plunged his bayonet right into guy's stomach! I saw this many, many times at Buchenwald and at the camps that followed.

You had to keep your eyes on the ground in front of you. This was crucial. It was an important part of blending in. If you stuck out, you could get beaten or killed. It also was important because walking in the wooden soled shoes wasn't easy. You had to shuffle. Stumbling over something could get you killed.

Taking care of your shoes and feet was also very important because if you started to limp, or you couldn't keep up, you were a dead duck. If the shoe strings rotted, which of course they did, you had to keep an eye out for a stray piece of wire at the factory. If the leather edges got hard and started cutting into your feet, you might need to chew them soft or wrap your feet in rags. Bad shoes and bad feet cost countless prisoners their lives, especially on the marches. They just couldn't keep up. They'd slip farther and farther back toward the end of the column. This is where I heard most of the gunshots coming from.

I'm sorry that I'm telling you all this. Remember, I never wanted to talk about any of it. For over sixty years, I've held it in. I pushed it back. I'm over 80 years old, and I'm brought to tears as I tell you about this. As I write this, the ink on this page is getting smeared by them. Everyone keeps telling me that I need to tell it all, so future generations will know, so that we never forget. They keep telling me that maybe I'll find some kind of personal healing through talking about it. But, to tell you the truth, I'm not sure they know what they're talking about.

I've done pretty damn well for myself these past years of silence. Working hard to take care of my wife and children healed me plenty. Trying very hard to enjoy good food and good Scotch was decent medicine. So it may be important that I say all this so people won't forget, but at this stage, I don't think it's very healthy for me. I'll do it because I should. I owe it to my mother and siblings. But people need to stop telling me it's good for me. They mean well, but they don't know what the hell they're talking about. Forgive me. This was a difficult part to tell.

Chapter Ten

A Little Hope

What I've been describing was my life, day-after-day, night-after-night. I'd get to the factory and see that someone I'd been working beside wasn't there. I'd know he'd joined the corpses along the road. I'd get back to Block 15 and see that a guy from the next bunk was gone. I'd know that his body was somewhere along the road.

I felt the saddest for the guys who collapsed during a march and were dragged to the side of the road still alive. Those poor souls faced a long, slow death with the birds picking them apart until the end. When people collapsed near the gates at Buchenwald, they were not left there very long. I suppose the SS guards didn't want them cluttering up the front gate. These people, dead or alive, were moved on carts to the crematorium sheds.

As I've said, the SS were ruthless monsters, every last one of them. I've read about one who was so horrible he earned the infamous title of the "Hangman of Buchenwald." He was an SS master sergeant named, Walter Gerhard Martin Sommer. Her was especially fond of hanging prisoners from the trees in the nearby forest. He hanged them from their wrists tied behind their backs. The SS began referring to the forest as the "singing forest," from the screams of the hanging prisoners. Sommer was also said to have ordered two Austrian priests to be crucified upside-down. I didn't know about any of this at the time because it was a very large camp, and you only knew about what you actually saw.

Mentioning the Austrian priests being hanged brings up something I should explain further. Yes, there were thousands of Jews at Buchenwald, but there were also other kinds of people as well. There were priests, gypsies, political prisoners, and even some P.O.W.s like the Soviet soldiers I mentioned earlier.

One day after I'd been at the camp for about three or four months, sirens started sounding while we were working at the factory. We were told to hurry out of the factory and into the yard outside. Standing in the yard I heard the loud hum of airplanes getting closer and closer. Next there were tremendous explosions roaring from the far end of the factory.

It was a clear day. I looked up and saw bombers flying past. As the bombs fell they made a horrifying screaming sound. They began exploding all around us across the expansive yard. The German soldiers had retreated to the relative safety of bomb shelters. We were out there on our own. I jumped into one of the big bomb craters along with twenty or so other guys. Each blast sent a shock wave through my entire body. I remember a guy next to me yelled something like, "We should be safe! What are the chances of two bombs landing in the same place?" I thought, is he joking? If he was joking, this fella had one hell of a sense of humor. Here we were, starving Nazi prisoners, bellies down in a fresh bomb crater, with more and more bombs falling all around us. Joking or not, his logic sounded pretty good at the time. I stayed in the crater.

After about five minutes the bombers were gone. There were maybe 40 to 50 guys killed in that first bombing. I had a lot of questions about this new development, but there was no time to ask any of the guys about it. I couldn't hear very well anyway. Right away the Germans got us busy clearing away damaged areas of the factory. We worked all that day clearing debris.

My ears were still ringing when we got back to Block 15 that night. There I was finally able to ask about the bombing. Several of the guys were pretty well educated, at least compared to me. They knew from the stars on the planes that these had been U.S. bombers.

They said it was a good sign the U.S. was fighting the Germans and able to bomb places this deep inside Germany.

This gave us a little hope. Maybe if we could just hold out long enough, someday the Americans would come free us. Hope was good, but of course, the bombing also gave us another thing to worry about. Maybe one of the bombs might just land on me. To be honest I would have rather died that way than any of the many other horrible ways people were dying.

Over time there were more and more bombings of the factories around Buchenwald. The British and Americans tended to bomb during the daytime, while the Soviets bombed at night. Sometimes a guy in my bunk would wake me up and say, "The Soviets are bombing the factories! What if they miss and hit us?"

"Better to get blown up by the Soviets than to get pushed into the furnace!" I'd answer, before going back to sleep.

The Soviets would drop flares dangling from parachutes, which would light up the whole area around the factories. They were very good at night bombing, always hitting the area around the factories, and never hitting the camp. Maybe they knew the camp held many Red Army prisoners of war? I don't know. I was utterly exhausted; I slept right through most of the night bombings.

Today if I'm ever having trouble sleeping in a hotel bed, you know, because the pillows are different from what I have at home, I marvel at how easily sleep came in the camps. I was cold, sleeping on hard wood bunks, being eaten alive by lice, a bunch of guys snoring right in my ear, and bombs going off, and I'd sleep like a baby. When you're starving, being worked to death, and only getting a few hours of sleep every night, you can sleep through anything.

A bombing might shut down the factory for a week or so. It was amazing how fast the Germans could rebuild, you know, with so many laborers at their disposal. Then we'd see a single airplane flying very, very high overhead. I've heard they were looking to see if smoke had started flowing from the factory's smoke stacks again. If they saw that it was, within a day or so, another wave of bombers would hit the factory again.

The Germans began placing antiaircraft guns all around the factories. The sound of them firing made the bombing even more hellish for us out in the factory yard. As you know, what goes up also comes back down. Therefore both bombs and antiaircraft shells rained down upon the factory and the yard.

To avoid the antiaircraft guns the bombers started flying higher and higher. In response the Germans came up with a trick of their own. If they had warning, I guess from plane spotters along the bombing route or radar, they would use some kind of chemical to produce artificial fog across the entire valley. There were these barrels, a little larger than an oil drum, spaced along the outside of the fence around the factory.

The sirens would go off, and we'd head out to the yard outside the factory. German men, regular citizens who worked at the factory, not soldiers, would run and open the lids of the barrels. Some type of artificial fog would start pouring out the barrels. The fog would form a thick cloud that would hide the factory from the approaching bombers. The cloud's bottom was about fifteen feet off the ground; the top was above the factory smoke stacks. It didn't stop the planes from dropping bombs, but it must have made it a little harder to pinpoint the factory.

So the Allies were bombing the German factories, and even though we had to dodge the bombs, all in all, it was a positive development. The Allies were fighting, and the bombs provided evidence of this on a regular basis. And I think here I should mention that we sometimes planned and carried out our own acts of war. In our own way, we did our own fighting. We had no weapons, but we were not entirely helpless. I've never told a living soul about this. I'm really not sure I should.

The first time was after we were fairly well settled in at Buchenwald. The kapo assigned to our barracks was a particularly cruel animal. He turned in a lot more guys than did most kapos. More times than not, it was for no reason at all. As I've explained, the punishment for being turned in was death by hanging at the gallows inside the main gate. This kapo also seemed to delight in kicking guys in the groin for no reason at all. We all hated him. Each night we talked about how horrible he was and that God should strike him dead.

One night a couple of the older guys decided that maybe we shouldn't wait for God. They suggested that the very next time the kapo came into the barracks at night, we should jump on him and smother him to death. The guys discussed this and decided two issues were very important. We couldn't leave any marks that could show he was beaten or strangled, and he must not be allowed to scream.

We talked about what the consequences of this might be and concluded the Germans would be practical. They still needed us for labor. Would it be easier for them to replace one kapo or a barracks full of laborers? As the youngest in the block, I did not participate in the attack. That being said, I was completely in favor of it.

Each night we waited for him to come in, which he often did. The night arrived, and we were ready. The kapo stepped in through the doorway and strolled down along the aisle between the rows of bunks. Just after he passed us, five or six of guys quietly slipped down from their bunks and rushed him. A couple of the biggest guys got to him first and one covered his mouth with both hands, as the others joined in pushing him to the hard wood floor. One guy shoved a shirt deep into the kapo's mouth. The guys sat atop him, pinning him to the floor. Between the shirt stuffed into his mouth and the weight of the guys on him, he couldn't breathe. In no time at all the kapo was dead.

They carefully carried his body to the door. One of the guys opened the door a crack and took a look around. After removing his green arm band, worn by all the kapos, two of the guys dragged the kapo's body outside and added it to the nearest pile of dead bodies.

Once back inside, a couple of the guys went from bunk-to-bunk spreading the word that no matter what, no one should rat out the guys involved. They probably didn't need to do this. Like I said, the camaraderie among the guys was unbelievable.

A day or two later the SS men came and asked where our kapo was. To a man, we all said that we didn't know. We said we hadn't seen him for a couple days. This time no one was punished. We simply got a new kapo. The new kapo was no saint, but he wasn't bad enough to kill.

Do I feel bad about this? No. The kapos were hardened criminals straight out of German prisons. They were the worst of the worst: murderers and rapists. This guy was getting good guys killed, not because they broke any rules, but simply because he was evil. We may not have been part of the military, but we were very much at war. He was our enemy. Killing him saved the lives of our guys. I've never lost a moment's sleep over it. Please don't judge us too harshly. As best you can, try put yourself in our place.

I felt proud of what we'd done. The Nazis had taken everything from us. They had total control over every aspect of our lives and terrorized us without ceasing. Killing the kapo was proof that in spite of all this, we had not been defeated; we were not helpless.

At Buchenwald, and at the other camps that followed, this was our only weapon against the worst of the kapos. We practiced it with utmost restraint, not out of any sense of morality, but rather because it was dangerous. Survival was our only concern. We weren't too worried about whether a certain kapo was worthy of a death sentence. Trust me they all deserved it. We couldn't do it too often, or the SS would surely catch on. When I say "we," I mean my fellow prisoners. The whole block was in on these acts. If caught, we were all equally likely to get killed. However, as far as the actual killings, only the largest, healthiest guys were involved. I was the youngest and among the smallest. Had I been larger, would I have actually done this? Would I have been able to shove a shirt down a kapo's throat? It's hard to say.

We did it once or twice in Buchenwald and at the other camps too. Most times we got away with it without punishment. Several times we did not. On these occasions, when the SS could not get any answers from the guys in the barracks, they'd pick out two or three of the older, weaker guys. They would tell them if they didn't say who killed the kapo, they would be shot.

Of course the guys who were picked never told. The SS would shout for everyone to line up outside. The two or three older guys would be lined up in front and given one more chance. Still they never talked. If I were in their place, I wouldn't have either. Each got a bullet in the head. This was horrible, but it never made us regret killing the kapo. The kapos we took out were getting three to four guys killed every week. What would you have done?

Chapter Eleven

Back into Poland

One morning, after I'd been at Buchenwald for about 12 or 13 months, when we were marching to work, we didn't stop at the factory. We marched on by. I thought maybe we're going to work at another factory a little farther away. But we kept on marching past all the factories and on out into the countryside. We marched for a few hours and then stopped to receive our usual bowl of rancid soup to eat. We started again and marched all day and into the evening. Along the way guys who couldn't keep up were killed by a rifle butt or a bullet to the head. Their dead bodies littered the roadside here and there along the way.

After four or five days we arrived at very large camp. It was every bit the size of Buchenwald. It looked pretty much like Buchenwald and Blechhammer: tall barbed wire fences, guard towers, and row after row of barracks. We entered through a stone archway. A tower with large windows sat atop the archway. The "*Arbeit Macht Frei*," (work sets you free) sign was prominently displayed above the archway. Another sign let us know the name of the camp, Gross-Rosen.

I didn't know until I spoke with the guys in the barracks that night, but at some point along the march we'd actually left Germany and reentered Poland. At the time I didn't care. Poland or Germany meant nothing to me. I was numb to such details. A camp was a camp. It was all the same.

Going from Buchenwald to Gross-Rosen has caused a bit of confusion among some of the Holocaust "experts" I've met. Apparently there were very well documented marches out of Blechhammer, which stopped for a time at Gross-Rosen on their way to Buchenwald. I, on the other hand, went from Blechhammer to Buchenwald and then back into Poland to Gross-Rosen. I'm not a Holocaust expert. That is, I didn't earn a Ph.D. at a fine university learning all about such things. However I was there. I can tell you beyond the shadow of a doubt; I went from Blechhammer to Buchenwald and then to Gross-Rosen. Maybe for a time there was a shortage of able workers at Gross-Rosen, so they sent us from Buchenwald? I can't tell you why, but I can tell you it happened.

There was one thing to be happy about in the new camp, and I use "happy" in a very, very light sense, because there truly wasn't happiness to be found in the camps. I couldn't see any crematorium smoke stacks. I thought, "Maybe they have them, but at least I don't have to look at them."

I've read that the camp was as large as Auschwitz, but of course I only saw one little part of it. After we passed through the gate, we immediately entered a large roll call yard. There we were sorted and assigned to barracks. I was assigned to Block 18, which was among the cluster of barracks back and to the right of the yard. Of course it was set up exactly like all my previous barracks.

I didn't know any of the guys in Block 18. Most were Polish and German Jews, so we shared Yiddish as a common second language. A couple of guys were from Hungary or elsewhere and didn't speak Yiddish. We'd all picked up little bits of various languages, including quite a bit of German along the way. Thus, no matter where a guy was from, I could communicate with him fairly well.

Life at Gross-Rosen was the same as the other camps. We woke before dawn, stood in the yard for roll call, left through the front gate, made a right onto the road in front of camp, and marched a few miles to work in a nearby factory. We worked all day, marched back to camp, waited in line for horrible bits of food, and collapsed into sleep.

Those who couldn't do this died. They died in their bunks. They died marching to or from work. They died on their own or with the help of an SS monster or kapo demon. They died everyday and every night. They died faster than they could be carted away to wherever they were taken at Gross-Rosen. The bodies of the dead and close to dead piled up in stacks everywhere.

I don't know what else to tell you about my time at Gross-Rosen. Every day was just like another, whether in Gross-Rosen or Buchenwald or wherever. There was one more little thing to be "happy" about at Gross-Rosen as compared with Buchenwald. For some reason or another, the Allies were not bombing the factories outside Gross-Rosen while I was there. So at least I didn't have to dodge falling bombs and antiaircraft shells while working at the factory.

I've done a little reading to learn more about Gross-Rosen. As I've said, I only really saw what was right in front of me. All kinds of things may have been going on elsewhere, but I only knew what I could see.

Gross-Rosen was located in Lower Silesia, which is now a part of Poland. It was constructed by slave labor in the summer of 1940 as a sub-camp of Sachsenhausen. Later, in May of 1941, it was designated as its own independent camp.

Initially labor efforts were focused on work at a very large stone quarry and the construction of the main camp. Eventually work included building 60 to 70 sub-camps, as well as labor at numerous factories. One the more famous of its sub-camps, located in the Czechoslovakian town of Brünnlitz, housed the Jews who were rescued by Oskar Schindler, made famous by the movie, *Schindler's List*.

Approximately 125,000 prisoners flowed through Gross-Rosen and its sub-camps during their existence. While I never saw a single female at Gross-Rosen, 500 female SS guards were trained there and served at some of its sub-camps.

What else can I say about Gross-Rosen? Life was tough. We were miserable. Many guys died while I was there, but somehow I survived. One day, after three or four months at Gross-Rosen, I thought we were marching to work, but instead we kept going. The guys around me immediately began whispering the usual questions, "Where are we going?" "What's going to happen to us?"

Chapter Twelve

A Return to Germany

After about five or six days of marching, we turned onto a road that wound its way uphill through heavy woods. The fresh smell of the pines gradually gave way to the all too familiar smell of death. Eventually we arrived at a camp. A sign at the gates let us know we'd arrived at Flossenbürg. The camp sat atop a 1,500 meter high mountain near the Austrian-Czech border. It was similar to the other camps in terms of barbed wire fences, guard towers, and barracks. As with Gross-Rosen, I didn't see any crematorium buildings at the camp. I learned later that indeed there was a crematorium facility, but thankfully it was separate from the camp.

I've recently seen an old photograph of the camp and nearby town. Looking at the photograph, I was startled to see a castle perched atop a prominent stone outcropping. It sits high above the camp and would have dominated the view from anywhere in the area. I have absolutely no memory of ever seeing it! Every day as I walked out the front gate on the march to work, it would have been easily visible just off the left. This unseen castle serves as a perfect example of just how incredibly warped my life had become living for years in the camps.

This is difficult to understand if you haven't been in a camp or on a march. First of all, you're wearing wooden soled shoes. You have to shuffle along, and you have to concentrate on every step, through rain or snow, to make sure you don't slip. If you slip and fall, you could hurt yourself and that could cost you your life. If you slip and fall, even if you don't hurt yourself, you attract attention. You don't want attention. Secondly, just the simple act of looking around could get you noticed. So everywhere you go, everything you do, you keep your head down.

Even so, I do I remember seeing a lot of smoke rising up from an area of the forest behind the camp. Guys had asked around about it and learned there were no factories off in that direction. I later learned that a very strange type of crematorium was the source of the smoke at Flossenbürg. On a hillside behind the camp, a giant pit was excavated in the forest. A roaring fire was maintained at the bottom of the pit. Bodies were loaded all across a large grate made of iron bars that was set above the fire. Bodies were also placed on a second grate set above the first. Why the Germans constructed this horrifying crematorium, as opposed to those used elsewhere, I have no idea.

I was assigned to Block 22 and shared my bunk with two or three guys. Life at Flossenbürg was very much like it had been at the other camps. Every day was the same. We woke very early in the morning for roll call. If a guy was having trouble standing, an SS soldier would brutally beat him and take him away to be killed. We marched two to three miles to a factory. I worked moving boxes from one part of the factory to another, never knowing what was in them or what was being produced. They gave us a bowl of garbage to eat, and we continued to work into the evening. Then we marched back to camp, maybe got another bowl of soup, and went to sleep.

I should explain a little bit about getting our evening meal. It was more or less the same at every camp. On most days we'd arrive back from work at about nine o'clock. The trucks with the food pots would pull up near our barracks, and we'd stand in line for about an hour. Each of us had a spoon, which we carefully kept in a pocket in the side of our pants. We also had a metal bowl, which was hung by a string from our necks. If you had a belt, sometimes you'd hang it from your belt. When you finally got to the front of the line, a kapo would dip a ladle into a big pot and pour the foul, watery broth into your bowl. At last you would find a place to sit on the ground and eat your meager meal. If you were unlucky enough to be at the end of the line, some-times there was nothing left.

As I've stressed to you, in the camps you always had to be very careful with each and every step. I was never more careful than dur-ing the brief time between holding out my cup to receive food and sitting down to eat. One little stumble, one little accidental bump from another guy, and you could spill your meal. If you spilled your bowl, it was your bad luck. You wouldn't get another. What little we ate was not enough to keep us going. We were all slowly starving to death. You couldn't risk the loss of even one little bowl of water-soaked cabbage leaves or other such scraps.

Aside from the fear of spilling your bowl, the time of the evening meal was the closest we came to relaxing. The SS and kapos didn't bother us during this time. I guess they knew we had one thought and only one thought on our minds: getting and eating our food. So they backed off a bit and relaxed. This allowed us to let down our guard as well. In the food line we'd chat with each other a bit, "What kind of shit will they give us tonight?" was the most common question.

We could even share a little bit of humor as long as we kept it quiet. A guy might say, "I heard we're getting a nice beef brisket with baked potato tonight. The fat kapo over at Block 10 choked on a sau-sage this morning. They didn't want all that good meat to go to waste, so they sliced him up. There was enough for every guy in the camp to get a nice chunk of brisket!" Of course there was no brisket, just a wa-tery soup with a few wilted vegetable leaves mixed in.

Once seated on the ground, with my bowl of soup safely in my hands, I'd slowly take in each and every bite. I recently read about a British P.O.W. who switched places with a Jewish prisoner and snuck into a work camp at Auschwitz. He actually did this twice, each time spending the night inside a barracks. I mention this because the P.O.W., who was extremely malnourished himself, could not bring himself to eat the awful soup being fed the Jewish prisoners. He said the smell was so horrible it turned his stomach. But this, and some-times a chunk of hard, black bread, was all we had. I probably could-n't eat it today, even if you paid me a million dollars. But back then I got used to it. It was a simple choice: eat or starve.

Once the bowl was empty, I'd carefully lick every last bit of moisture from my bowl and spoon. Then I'd get up and stand in line to use the little water spigot outside the barracks. I'd quickly get a drink and wash my bowl and spoon. Lastly a siren would sound indicating it was time to return to the barracks for sleep. As I've mentioned, we'd chat a little in the bunks and quickly fall to sleep. After a few short hours, the sirens would go off again. Each and every morning I'd hear the siren, open my eyes and think, "Oh, I'm still alive."

While I was at Flossenbürg the factories were not being bombed. Also I didn't live right next to the crematorium. I was barely surviving, and guys were dying left and right from disease and starvation. But at least I didn't have to dodge bombs or watch live people being shoved into ovens. I don't mean to make light of this fact. It was a very big deal to me. Life was horrible, yet it was so much better than back at Buchenwald.

I've read that Flossenbürg was established in 1938 and initially held about 1,600 prisoners. It is estimated that over 111,000 prisoners were held in the main camp and its numerous sub-camps over the course of the war. I hesitate to throw all these facts and figures at you. My fear is that with such large numbers it's easy to forget that each prisoner was a real person, just as I am, with a name and a family. I was just one of the 111,000 prisoners who flowed through Flossenbürg. We must remember that each and every one of these prisoners had his own story. As many as 73,000 prisoners died or were murdered there. I have children, grandchildren, and great-grandchildren; I cherish them with all my heart. These 73,000 individuals never had the opportunity to do the same.

Why did I survive? Only God knows. Yes, I was large for my age; otherwise I would have been killed right away. And yes, I'd grown up with a cruel father, and that prepared me to live under the rule of kapos and SS guards. And truly I was blessed with a great deal of energy and endurance. However random chance played an equally strong role in who survived and who perished. Some guys got stabbed or shot for no apparent reason. I smarted-off to a guard and got away with only a gun butt to my chin. So I wasn't any smarter or stronger than the 73,000 prisoners who never walked out of Flossenbürg.

About 40,000 prisoners were there in 1945. Between April 1944 and April 1945, additional gallows were installed, and over 1,500 prisoners were hanged. The crematorium facility could not keep up with the number of deaths from execution, disease, and starvation.

The SS began stacking the bodies in piles, pouring gasoline over them, and setting them on fire.

In September of 1944 Flossenbürg, like Gross-Rossen, became a training center for female guards. This was very unusual. Throughout my years at all the camps, and all the marches, I'd never seen a single female guard. I never saw one at Flossenbürg. Apparently they were trained at Flossenbürg and then sent to its various sub-camps.

There's not much more I can tell you about my time at Flossenbürg. Life was horrible. The war was wearing on and on. The camps were becoming more and more crowded. People seemed to be dying faster and faster. Somehow I survived. I thought of my mother and siblings every day. When I was waiting at roll call, trying to stand still and straight, I'd remember bouncing little Rosie on my knee, making her laugh with an occasional tickle. While chewing the hard, tasteless bread, I'd think about the glorious smell of the stews and baked goods at the bakery. While marching to work in blinding snow, I'd think of sledding with Majer. And always, always I'd think of my dear mother – the queen of all mothers.

After about one year at Flossenbürg, we marched off to work and just kept going.

Chapter Thirteen

The Train

When we stopped for the night, we had another bowl of awful soup and slept in an open field. The guys quietly began with their endless questions, "I guess we're leaving Flossenbürg, where are we going?" "What's going to happen to us?" And of course the Germans had told us nothing. They hadn't even told us that we were leaving Flossenbürg.

The march continued on for two or three days; I can't remember exactly. Then we came to a little village where a train was waiting for us. The Germans loaded us onto cattle cars. We were crammed in, but there was just enough room to sit down. The cars were fairly well ventilated, with a little air coming in from the space between the wooden slats of the walls. However the train never stopped. We had to go to the bathroom in the car. As always some guys were sick with diarrhea. The floor and air became utterly disgusting. When a guy died the people near him would take turns sitting on his body. This may seem heartless, but please try to understand. It was better than sitting in urine and excrement.

I was able to sleep a little here and there on the train, leaned up against other guys. The monotonous clickety-clack of the train lulled me to sleep. After a number of hours I was jolted awake by the roar of low-flying planes. Suddenly all hell broke loose from the skies.

Through the openings between the slats, I saw small planes buzzing the train. They began dropping bombs: one from under each wing. The train engine must have been hit because the train came to an abrupt stop, throwing us hard against each other and the floor of the train. Fortunately I was not injured.

The SS guards ran away from the train, but they hadn't bothered to lock the doors. The planes started firing their machine guns, and prisoners were getting shot through the roof and sides of the box cars. We were trapped, and for a brief moment no one moved. If we stayed inside, we'd get killed. However the Nazis had crushed our spirits so thoroughly we were reluctant to open the doors.

As the planes came by for another pass, a tall prisoner near the door took the initiative. He started to slide the door open and other guys soon jumped forward to help. Within seconds we were out of the car. The same thing was happening up and down the train. Thousands of prisoners were scrambling to get away from the train. The planes were coming in very low. I could see the stars painted on them, which I knew meant they were American.

It was frightening, yet exciting! Just as you hear about, time truly seemed to slow down. I was moving away from the train as fast as I could. A guy tripped and fell in front of me. I stopped to help him up, and as I did I remember pausing just a moment to look all around. There was so much to take in, and for that brief second it was safe to raise my head and look all around! I was in grave danger from the bombs and bullets, but I could look around without fear of being hit by a kapo. It was wonderful! Dark smoke was billowing up from the engine. American planes were zipping past overhead, their engines screaming, and machine guns blasting. Though I was caught square in the middle of battle, for that brief moment I didn't care. It was exhilarating! I've never felt so alive. But I wasn't crazy. In a flash I was right back at it, shuffling as fast as my wooden soled feet could carry me.

The pilots must have recognized that we were prisoners because we were all wearing the striped pajama looking clothes. They stopped firing and flew off as quickly as they'd come. I have a great love for the American soldiers. Obviously they thought our train was a German supply train. They had no way of knowing we were trapped inside. I hope those brave pilots never lost a night of sleep over accidently killing some of us.

We were all dying anyway. At the time I was just hoping to make it through that day. The Allies were our only hope. They needed to bomb factories and supply trains to win the war. Many people think they should have bombed the concentration camps as well. They believe that although many people would have been killed by the bombs, knocking out the camps may have actually saved lives in the long run. I don't know if that would have saved lives. I'd seen firsthand how the Germans didn't need camps to kill people. Forcing starving people to march for hours on end worked all too well.

Once the planes flew off, in no time at all, the SS men rounded us up. Since the bombs had destroyed the train engine and several of its cars, our only option was to march. Some guys were accidently killed in the bombing. Many others died during the march. We were accustomed to all manner of death, so it didn't bother us. But I wonder how the plane attack may have affected the SS soldiers. They were used to wielding complete power. They were the ones who dished out pain and death. The American pilots had just challenged their power. I don't recall noticing anything different about them. However you never looked directly at an SS man's face, so at the time I couldn't make such judgments.

Thinking about it now, I hope the attack put great fear deep into their hearts. I like the thought of the fear of death eating away at them as they marched alongside our column of filthy, starving prisoners. Fear would have been new for them; however, we'd long since become used to living with it every moment. I hope it ate at them for the rest of their lives. This may sound harsh or vindictive. However I can't apologize. This is how I feel. I don't hold a grudge against the German people or even the *Wehrmacht* soldiers. God judges each man, so I leave this to him. But I'm talking specifically about the SS. They were heartless beasts.

After two and a half days we arrived at another camp. There was a large eagle statue at the front gate, as well as the "*Arbeit macht frei*," (Work will set you free) sign. Another sign read, "Dachau." I'm sure the Germans thought it was all very impressive. To me it was just another camp.

Chapter Fourteen

Dachau

Except for the eagle, Dachau looked pretty much the same as Blechhammer, Buchenwald, Gross-Rosen, and Flossenbürg. To "normal" people I'm sure there were a hundred obvious things that made Dachau seem very different from all the others. But to me, at that time, it was just another camp. Shuffling through the gate, I thought it might be worse than Buchenwald, or it might be a little better. Either way, it didn't matter all that much. All I knew was that I'd arrived at a camp. That night I'd sleep in a barracks. Tomorrow I probably wouldn't be forced to march all day.

On our way to the front gate we'd passed a section outside the main camp devoted to the barracks and offices of the SS. I noted this only because had I been younger, like so long ago back in Jeleśnia and Blechammer, I would have been assigned to work there.

The prisoner section of camp was encircled by three formidable layers. The outer consisted of tall barbed wire fences and watch towers spaced evenly along the perimeter. The middle layer was an electrified fence. Finally the inner-most layer was a ditch or moat half filled with putrid smelling water. Again I'm sure the Germans were all very proud of all this. Its dark grandeur was lost on me, however. At this point of the war, I'd seen so much. I'd been through so much. I merely wanted to sit down and maybe get a little bowl of soup.

Immediately inside the eagle and front gate was a rectangular roll call yard, with another of equal size directly beside it. To the left of each yard, with a single narrow road running between them, were two identical rows of barracks.

My section of our long column of exhausted prisoners stopped at the second roll call yard. We assembled in rows and were assigned to barracks. My barracks was somewhere in the middle, along the row of barracks to the right of the road which divided the camp. Maybe it was from fatigue, or perhaps I'd simply stopped caring at this point, but I don't remember the number of the barracks I was assigned to at Dachau.

I've read that horrible, unspeakable medical experiments were conducted in the fifth barracks along the row I was assigned to; thankfully I knew nothing of this at the time. I've read about these experiments, and perhaps you've heard a bit about them as well. Thank God they are not directly a part of my story. Therefore I will say nothing more of them.

I didn't know at the time, but Dachau was the first concentration camp in Germany and served as a model from which all other camps were constructed. It opened on March 22, 1933. This was just 51 days after Hitler came to power. It was planned out by Commandant Theodor Eicke, who went on to become the chief inspector of all concentration camps. He made sure they were all built and run according to his design. This perhaps explains why all the camps, with the exception of Jeleśnia, looked very similar.

And of course the SS didn't give us a grand tour of the place. I only saw what I saw, you know, what was right in front of me. But apparently, aside from the SS section, the camp had two main areas: prisoner barracks and a crematorium. Thankfully my barracks wasn't anywhere near the crematorium.

The camp was originally built as a prison for political prisoners, but it later held a variety of people. For instance Dachau was Germany's main camp for holding Christian prisoners. About 3,000 Catholic deacons, priests, and even bishops were imprisoned there.

Conditions there were every bit as bad as at Buchenwald, Gross-Rosen, and Flossenbürg. With the Allies squeezing in at the Germans from all sides, camps inside of the German homeland were becoming horribly overcrowded. Because of overcrowding, we only stayed at Dachau for about ten days. There simply wasn't any room. I think that after the train was bombed they didn't know what to do with us. Perhaps they marched us to Dachau only because it was the closest option. And then they kept us there until they could figure out someplace else to keep us.

I've read that the commandant at Dachau had been begging his superiors to stop sending more prisoners. He was concerned the typhus epidemics that were sweeping the camp might get out of hand. They might spill outside and infect the German population. At the time of the liberation of Dachau, about 200 prisoners were dying every day from disease and starvation.

Since we were only at Dachau for such a short while, they didn't assign us to a work detail. The siren would sound each morning, and the regular prisoners of the camp would assemble in the yards and then head off to work. We didn't need to assemble for roll call, but the kapos watched us and kept an accurate count.

After the resident prisoners left for work, we were free to hang out in the barracks or walk around the yards. Most of the time, we slept. Our time at Dachau was no cake walk; everyday people from my group from Flossenbürg were still dying. That never stopped. And the bodies of the dead and almost dead from across the entire camp were piled up here and there. For our group, however, Dachau gave us a chance to rest and recuperate as best we could. We were so happy we didn't have to assemble for roll call and march off to work. As I've described, roll call and marching to and from work were very dangerous times.

And instead of getting by with just a few hours of sleep, we could sleep as much as we wished. Our bodies and minds were utterly exhausted. The sleep was an incredible luxury, which undoubtedly helped prepare me for what was still to come.

We were fed the usual garbage once or twice a day. Trucks made to run on burning wood brought the food to our group of barracks and parked along the road that separated the two sides of camp.

I didn't see much of the camp, mainly just the barracks and the yard. We weren't watched very closely while we wandered around the yard, so I was able to actually look up and around without fear of getting hit or shot. As I stood in the yard, facing the two rows of barracks, I could see a constant flow of smoke rising up from an area directly outside and to the left of the back section of our camp. Of course I knew this must be the crematorium.

I could hear the rolling thunder of bombs far off in the distance, but none fell anywhere close to Dachau while we were there. I didn't know it at the time, but these bombing runs were different than those I'd dodged at Buchenwald. Before the Allies were bombing factories, trying to impede Germany's ability to support the war effort. Now they were bombing German troops and installations, softening the homeland's defenses before the advancing American Army. Oh, how I wish I'd known that at the time! It would have given me much strength.

I'm so very sorry to have dragged you through all this. Most Holocaust survivor stories last only a year or so. Those are painfully too long for both those who lived through it and those who read their stories, page-by-horrible page.

You happen to take on the story of a survivor who had the terrible luck to be rounded up so very young. My story spans the entire war. I should have made this a little more clear at the beginning. It only would have been fair for you to know what you were getting yourself into. But then again, when I was put on that truck outside our little apartment in Bedzin, I didn't know what lay ahead either. But please stay with me. The horror doesn't last forever.

Honestly I actually feel a sense of guilt and shame over my experience at Dachau. I've been told not to feel this way, but I do. I have dear friends, fellow survivors at the St. Louis Holocaust Museum, who were long-term prisoners there. Their experience at Dachau was every bit as horrific as anything I'd been through at my camps.

That's something very strange about hearing or reading survivor stories. On the surface they may appear to hold contradictions, e.g., one survivor said Dachau was restful, another it was hell. Sadly these "contradictions" serve to fuel the bogus arguments of today's Holocaust deniers. In truth, however, they make perfect sense. Take a given camp such as Dachau. Surely the experience of a political prisoner during the camp's opening in the spring of 1933 would have been drastically different from any prisoner held there in the spring of 1945.

The experience among two prisoners held at the very same time, separated only by a few barracks, could have been vastly different. You'll recall that medical experiments were being conducted in the fifth barracks along the right side of the road that led between the two rows of barracks at Dachau. Let's say for instance that I was housed in the sixth barracks along that same row. I was somewhere along this area, but I honestly don't recall the number of my barracks. However let's just assume for a moment I was in the sixth.

The story of a survivor from the fifth barracks, someone being tortured in Nazi "medical" experiments, would be very different from mine. And let's say the seventh barracks, the one to the other side of mine, housed guys who'd lived and worked at Dachau for over a year. Their stories, each horrible and true, would be completely different from mine, as well as from the prisoner undergoing medical torture.

Just as your life is unique, intricately different from that of your next door neighbor, so was each survivor's experience. The guy in the bunk right next to me came from a different family. He may have stayed at different camps. His liberation may have unfolded differently from mine, as did his recovery, and his life after the camps. There was no "cookie-cutter" Holocaust experience. It was a very complex fabric woven from countless threads.

The SS were still at the camp. Therefore the Allies must have been a long way off. A bit later, as the SS saw the writing on the wall, they disappeared from the camps. The SS were the elite of the camp system. They were better informed than the regular soldiers and the kapos. When they knew the end was near, they fled the camps. Many shed their uniforms and tried to blend in with the civilian population.

There are reports that some of the soldiers who liberated Dachau were so incredibly upset and angry with what they found they rounded up and shot some of the guards. Other reports said the soldiers lent their rifles to prisoners allowing them to take vengeance on their tormenters. This was a rare occurrence. The vast majority of American soldiers did not do these sorts of things. Although, given that these soldiers had fought and clawed their way across every inch of France and Germany, one can hardly fault them for their actions.

The incidents were later investigated, but no soldiers were charged. This is as it should be. These soldiers had been through the hell of war before they came upon the camps. They were not prepared for what they found. They'd maybe heard mention that concentration camps were being liberated, but they didn't know at all what they were. If some lost their heads and killed some of the guards, was it wrong? I suppose in a perfect world acts like that wouldn't happen.

But was it wrong at Dachau in 1945? I can't find fault with them. I hope the soldiers who were involved never lost sleep over it.

On about the tenth day the SS marched us out the front gate. We marched for two or three days. During breaks and each night, as usual, the guys kept asking the same old questions. I thought that maybe we were heading back in the direction of Flossenbürg, as for a time the area seemed familiar. Then we turned and headed off in a different direction, so I had no idea where we were heading. A different direction could mean something or it could mean nothing. It could be terrible, or it could be slightly less than terrible. At this point I'd long since stopped worrying. I was numb. I just kept my eyes on the patch of ground immediately before my shuffling feet, and I kept marching.

Chapter Fifteen

Things Are Coming to an End

To this day I don't know where they were marching us. I've been told it was what has been termed, "a march to nowhere," meaning at this stage they just wanted to march us to death. During a break some of the older guys talked a little with a *Wehrmacht* guard. The guard told them, "Things are coming to an end." At the time I understood it to mean that we were going to be killed soon. They were going to march us to a mass grave someplace, and after all this, they'd kill me with a bullet to the head.

On the first night, which may have been April 20, we marched in darkness long after the sun set. Finally we collapsed to the ground and slept. We did the same on the following days and nights. Each morning I awoke thinking, "Oh, I'm still alive. I guess 'the end' wasn't last night." I was hungry, but I'd been starving for six years. The extra sleep at Dachau had really helped, so I felt like I could march like this for as many days as they made us.

Not everyone was doing as well. Guys continued to drop off to the side or couldn't keep up, slowly falling back in the column toward the rear. Gunshots came at regular intervals from the back of the column. The crack of each gunshot was like an alarm going off in my head. I'd think, "That's not going to be me. Keep going. Stay strong."

Early in the morning on April 23 it started to rain. At 10 o'clock we were marching downhill along a road outside Cham, Germany. Through the pouring rain, I saw two tanks appear over the top of a hillside off to the left. I said, "*Oy gavalt,*" which means, "Oh my God!" I didn't know who in the hell it was. I looked at the tanks and thought; "Maybe they are going to use their machine guns." After six years of trying so hard to stay alive, I thought this is where it was going to end. I'd end up just like all the others I'd seen over the years: just one more dead body along some God forsaken road.

Then we could see men marching behind the tanks and we could tell they were wearing green uniforms. Some guys yelled, "It's the Americans!" And that was pure joy!

The Germans who were guarding us (*Wehrmacht,* with maybe only one or two SS men) began running into the forest off to the right side of the road. The tanks rushed over there and began blasting into the woods with their flame throwers. It was quite a sight. I stood in dumbstruck delight and watched. Within a short time the Germans came walking out of the woods with their hands in the air. The American soldiers rounded them up and made them sit together on the ground.

As the combat troops continued moving forward with the tanks, support units arrived. The American soldiers came up and started telling us things in English. I spoke Polish and Yiddish (also German, Hungarian and bits of other languages), but not a word of English. One of the guys came over, and I'll never forget the guy's name, Israel Freidman. And he said to me in Yiddish, "What's your name?" He was Jewish! I couldn't believe it. I'd thought a great deal about the American soldiers, but I just never imagined that some of them were Jewish.

I blurted out, "Bendet. My name is Bendet!" He told me that I was safe now. I was going to be okay. I sat down in the wet grass utterly and completely stunned. Was this a dream? My heart was filled with overflowing joy, but my head took a little while to catch up. For six long years I'd thought of one thing, and one thing only, staying alive. Over and over, every moment of every single day, I repeated the same thoughts "Keep your eyes down. Keep your mouth shut. Keep working. Keep walking."

Then in a heartbeat it was over. The horror was over. I was free! I was free to look up at the sky. I could look directly at people. I could look right into the eyes of this wonderful American soldier named Israel Friedman. I could do all this, and nobody was going to hit me in the chin with a rifle. Nobody was going to put a bullet in my head. It was a wonderful moment! My heart was singing, but my mind was spinning.

I sat and watched in amazement as the Germans were loaded onto trucks. They'd loaded my family onto trucks, and now it was their turn. The American soldiers were firm, definitely and efficiently in charge, but they treated their German prisoners with respect. The Americans treated us like kings! They gave us cigarettes and what-ever food they had with them. We shook and kissed their hands and thanked them over and over.

I hesitate to tell you this next part because we're finally through with the horror. There was one last and terrible problem that happen-ed all of a sudden. We didn't expect it, nor did the brave Americans. To our mutual dismay we soon discovered it can be deadly for starv-ing people to eat too much food, too fast.

I would say that anywhere between 200 to 300 guys died from eating too fast. Their stomachs couldn't take it. Within 20 to 30 min-utes guys were doubling over with cramps. One-by-one they began dying all around us. It was unbelievable. We had survived. We were finally safe. And now this – it was horrifying. Can you imagine? They'd survived the Germans only to be done in by overeating.

I've asked a couple doctors about this, how eating too much could kill you. They put it this way. You know how if you're laid up in bed for a really long time and your muscles get all skinny and weak? When you're starving, your stomach and intestines can get that way too. The lining gets very weak and thin. And you also have bacteria that live down there, and they haven't been doing very well because you're not sending down much food and water. Then, all at once, you're dumping a bunch of both down into your system.

This stretches your weak and thin lining even further, and pro-vides a feast to all the bacteria. They start to multiply. It creates a population boom among all the normal bacteria that live down there, plus given the filthy conditions you've been living in, God knows what else is down there. The lining doesn't necessarily split, but it's thin enough for the bacteria to pass on through into your blood system.

These bacteria may not do you much harm hanging out in your intestines, but they are lethal when loosed into the rest of your system.

I thank God I didn't eat as fast as those poor guys. I don't know how I knew to take it slowly. Of course part of me wanted to eat as much as I could. I wanted very badly to stop the hunger I'd lived with for so long. What would I have done to get a little chunk of beef had such a thing been available in the camps? Now there were whole cans of beef right in front of me. All I had to do was reach out and take them. But some instinct was stronger than the hunger. It told me to take it slowly.

One day you're facing death, and now the miracle has happened. It's...I could never adequately describe the feeling to you. It's impossible. Can you imagine six years of horror? Some days I was hoping the Allied bombs will kill me. That would at least put an end to my suffering. How I survived is beyond me. The Germans had convinced themselves that I was an animal. They believed I was less than human. But they were wrong. They were so very, very wrong.

In thinking that we were less than human, the Germans had lost their own humanity. They'd become animals. They'd treated us like animals, but this had not snuffed out our humanity. Living in filth and unspeakable brutality hadn't polluted our hearts. We treated each other with respect. We encouraged each other, even daring to steal bits of food for each other.

Now the Americans were there, and they were treating us like humans. This confirmed what we'd known deep in our souls. We were indeed fully and wonderfully human. And now we were free! The only way I can describe it to you, it's like being born into a new world.

The freedom that we had when we were liberated was indescribable. Maybe some people have the words in their vocabulary, but I don't because it's too hard to describe. I was never a kid. Instead, I was a prisoner. I was 9 years old, 10 years old, 11, 12, 13 14, 15, every moment, every day, every year - a prisoner. And then, in the rain, the pouring rain, I was liberated. Freedom, what an incredible, wonderful gift! And you have it too! I beg of you, please, please don't take this gift for granted. Cherish it. Relish in it. Protect it. Try never to abuse it.

Chapter Sixteen

Treated Like a King

The Americans carefully loaded us into their trucks, which were similar to the trucks the Germans had used to take us away in back in 1939. Oh, what a different feeling I had on this ride!

We rode to the nearby village of Cham. In a matter of hours the Americans transformed this quiet little village into a fully operational center for survivors. The soldiers set up tents with cots for us to rest on. Guys who needed it most were given medical care. Now that the Americans knew better, they took great care to make sure we didn't eat too much food.

I spoke with Israel Friedman for hours. He was a sergeant serving with the U.S. Army Signal Corps. Israel was from Brooklyn, New York, and back home he had a wife and two kids. His parents were first-generation Americans who'd come from Poland.

Prior to arriving in Cham, Israel spent some time at Buchenwald immediately after its liberation. He didn't tell me much about what he'd seen there. He asked me about all I'd been through, and he couldn't believe it. It made his eyes tear up.

When he learned that I was alone, and most likely an orphan, Israel offered to adopt me! He explained that he didn't know how to do it right away, but that if I was willing, he'd find a way. I thought about his incredibly kind offer for a moment. It was very tempting. He was a fine gentleman, and even in our backward little town of Bedzin we'd heard about New York City. Perhaps I should have jumped at the opportunity, but I told him I needed to try my best to find out if anyone in my family had survived. He understood, but he gave me his name and contact information in case I changed my mind.

One day Israel introduced me to a very unusual soldier. Sadly I can't remember his name; but I will never forget him. He was a black rabbi serving as a chaplain with Israel's division! First of all, he was the very first black person I'd ever seen. I'd never heard there were black people, but his color didn't surprise, nor particularly interest me. Rather, I was very surprised to see a rabbi in the American Army. I've learned there were 790 black American chaplains serving during World War II. There were 311 rabbis. This man may have been the one and only black rabbi. I've tried to find out more about him, but I've had no luck.

I believe he was Hasidic, and under normal circumstance would have worn a long beard and side-lock curls. However, as an Army chaplain, he was clean shaven and wore his hair in the standard military cut. When you're only 15, it's difficult to judge the age of grown men. My best guess is that he was 40 to 45 years old.

The rabbi didn't speak Yiddish, and I didn't speak English. Israel served as our interpreter as the three of us talked many times over several days. The rabbi was from Brooklyn. That's really all I remember about him. He was intensely interested in learning about what I'd experienced and asked many, many questions. I wish I'd asked him a little more about himself. It would have been fascinating to learn how a black kid from Brooklyn ended up a Jewish rabbi.

The rabbi and Israel asked me a lot of questions about my family. I told them all about my wonderful mother, Majer, Rosie, and the baby. Also I told them a little about my father. They seemed to understand my strong desire to stay in Germany to search for family members. The rabbi said a special blessing asking God to watch over me and keep me strong during my search.

It was during this talk that I was given a very wise piece of advice. It may have come from the rabbi, or perhaps it was Israel, I honestly don't remember. Either way, the words came out of Israel's mouth, as he was interpreting. "Bendet, you've had a wonderful mother and a lousy father. You can't change that. Young men, and even old men, must look at the kind of people their parents are, and ask, over and over again, 'What is good about them? And what is bad?'

"Humans have a very strong tendency to behave as their parents. For men, we tend to take after our fathers. Who you are, is not set in stone. You are not destined to become your father. You are free to become anyone you'd like. But you must take great care in deciding who you should be. And that is only the start. Then every day you must work hard to become that person. Otherwise, if you simply go about your business, and never give this a thought, human nature will win out. Do you understand?"

At the time, of course, I got the gist of what was said. I replied that I understood. However this advice stuck with me throughout my entire life. I would come to understand it in a much deeper way over the years. Living a good life is hard work. It's easy to become lazy, to slide into bad habits. So don't. Wake up every morning and ask yourself what kind of person were you the day before? How can you do better today?

That first week, I think it was on Friday, the soldiers, Red Cross, and Jewish Family Services held a prayer service in Cham. There was a rabbi among them, and there was also a priest. I didn't understand what they were saying, but none-the-less it was a deeply moving experience. They say there are no atheists in fox holes; but, I don't know if that holds true for Nazi camps. It's very hard to understand how a loving God could allow so much senseless suffering. People tended toward one of two paths: intense atheism or intense faith.

I never saw a single person openly praying in the camps. Of course that doesn't mean we weren't. I prayed in my mind quite a bit. There's an old Irish proverb, "If God sends you down a stony path, may he give you strong shoes." Good or bad shoes often made the difference between life and death in the camps and during the marches. I can't remember if I prayed to God and properly thanked him for my good shoes while I was in the camps. I can tell you that I've thanked him many times since. You may think, "What's with this Polish Jew quoting Irish proverbs?" Keep reading. Anyway it was great to be free and able to openly pray with all these different kinds of people. It was very moving.

In time the Red Cross and Jewish Family Services took over. The soldiers had done an amazing job getting everything set up and taking great care of us. The Red Cross and Jewish Family Services did so as well. They arranged for me to stay at the home of a local German widow.

She'd lost her husband and two sons in the war. There were framed photos of each in uniform displayed across the mantle of her fireplace. I noted that one of her sons had the SS insignia on his uniform. Of course I didn't say anything about that. That would have been impolite. She had a little clothing store on the first floor of her home. I stayed in my own room, with my own bed, on the second floor above the shop. It felt nice to be around her clothing shop. It reminded me of home. She was a very kind and beautiful lady who treated me like her own son.

I'll never forget seeing my reflection for the first time in a mirror at her home. I hadn't seen myself for six years. Even though I saw everyday how terrible the guys around me looked, I guess I still had a mental picture of myself that looked like a 9 ½ year old boy. It stopped my breath. I just stood there in disbelief trying to square the image I saw in the mirror with the one I'd held in my head for six years. I started to feel sick. I broke out in a sweat and thought I might throw up. But then I told myself, "Be strong. It's over. Look at yourself. This is the worst you will ever look." I made the decision not to dwell on it. And that was that.

Also I'll never forget the first night sleeping in a regular bed, with a pillow, and nice clean sheets! For six years I'd slept in filth: my bedding and body infested with lice. This was a little bed, but I had the whole thing to myself; I didn't have some guy's stinking feet in my face. And some poor guy on his way out, too weak to make it to the outdoor latrines, wasn't fouling it with urine and excrement. I'm sorry to be so crude, but this is how things were. So it was very, very wonderful that at the nice lady's house, I had my own clean bed. It was heavenly. I got so excited; I had a hard time settling down to sleep!

The window of my little room overlooked a large community circle that served as the town center of Cham. Beautiful, colorful two and three story buildings lined the street of the circle. The town had not been damaged in the least during the war. Soldiers, trucks, and tents filled every inch of the circle. I slept with my window open to let in the clean fresh air. Each night I drifted off to sleep to the sounds of the wonderful American soldiers drinking, singing, and celebrating in the circle below. They must have found every bottle of beer, wine, and liquor in Germany! For the first time in six years I felt completely safe. An angelic lullaby from the very hosts of Heaven could not have sounded sweeter than their raucous celebration.

Local Germans donated clothing; thus I was very happy to say goodbye to my rotting striped pajama-like prison uniform and wooden soled shoes. I still had lice, but I was used to their torment. In the camps I could reach under my arm and scrape off a complete handful. Lice are tricky little bastards, and it actually took me about six months to get rid of all of them!

One day an American soldier came up to me with a huge smile. It turns out the day was May 8, 1945. He put his hands on my shoulders and said, "It's over! Germany has surrendered!" Another survivor, who spoke English and Yiddish, jumped for joy and shouted the good news in Yiddish.

I couldn't believe it! As word spread the survivors and soldiers broke out into a celebration that lasted all day and all night. The soldiers did quite a bit of drinking, dancing, and singing. I wish so badly I'd known English and that I'd taken up a liking for having a drink back then. I would have celebrated with those fine soldiers until the last bottle in Cham was dry! The local German citizens did not join in the celebration. They looked on passively.

I never heard this while recovering at Cham, but just six days after my liberation Hitler committed suicide. He put his pistol in his mouth and pulled the trigger. In the end had he changed his mind about the Jews? No. In the days just before his suicide, Hitler had been doing quite a bit of writing. He continued to blame Jews stating, "Centuries will go by, but from the ruins of our towns and monuments the hatred of those ultimately responsible will always grow anew against the people whom we have to thank for all this: international Jewry and its henchmen." He went on to say, "Above all, I enjoin the Government and the people to uphold the race laws to the limit and to resist mercilessly the poisoner of all nations, International Jewry." Hitler had wanted to kill me. He was dead; somehow I'd survived.

I only weighed about 70 pounds, but I was in pretty fair health. I didn't need any medical treatment, simply food and rest. At the camps sleep had been a precious commodity. You'd think I'd have slept in late every morning after liberation. I could have. I didn't have to do chores or march off to a factory. However I woke up early every morning. I still rise early even to this day. Maybe it's more important for me to catch up on being awake and truly alive, than it is for me to catch up on sleep. It's a lot more pleasant waking up wondering what to do today, than marveling that I'm not dead.

I did carry a couple of long-term health consequences from being starved in the camps. I lost all of my natural teeth during the first several years after liberation. I also believe my growth was stunted. I'd been very large for my age when I'd first been taken from Bedzin. You'll remember that is why I was able to pass for 15 ½ and avoided being killed right away. My father and his father both stood well above six feet tall. I, on the other hand, stopped growing at only about 5' 8."

After a little while the Military Police (M.P.) arrived and took control of things in Cham. I got to know an M.P., and one day I was chatting with him and admiring a number of M.P. motorcycles with side-cars. I can't remember if he offered to let me take one for a spin or if I asked. I probably asked. Either way, before I knew it, I was sitting atop the motorcycle, and the M.P. was giving me a quick lesson on how it all worked.

He asked if I was ready and made me promise to take it slowly and stay in town. Then I was underway! I couldn't believe it. I'd never felt so thrilled or so free! And yes, I was free. Clean, fresh air swept across my face. It felt wonderful, as if some of the filth from the camps was blown both off of me and out of me.

I drove the cycle around and around Cham gaining confidence as I went. Maybe I got to feeling a little too free because I took a corner a bit too fast and smashed the side-car right into the corner of a building! Fortunately the side-car broke free. I remained squarely on the cycle and continued past without a scratch and barely a wobble. I was a little nervous bringing the cycle back without the side-car, but the M.P. just laughed and laughed.

Every day I'd been thinking about my extended family and wondering who might have survived. Intellectually I knew there was almost no chance that my mother and siblings had made it. Emotionally, deep inside, I still held a small spark of hope. I thought it much more likely that I could locate a cousin or two.

After about four weeks in Cham, I awoke one morning and knew I was ready. It was time to begin looking for family members. I'd heard there were a large number of survivors staying in the town of Schomdorf. One of the local Germans gave me a bicycle, which I'd practiced riding all around Cham. After a quick breakfast I headed out for my first day of searching for relatives.

I peddled the bicycle about 10 kilometers and arrived in Schomdorf. The journey was a lot farther than my practice rides around Cham, but it sure beat marching. There were people out and about around a mar-ket in the center of town. I started asking if anyone knew any Fainers or Urmans. You won't believe this, but right away some guy said, "Yes. I know Rubin Fainer. He's right there," pointing to three men talking in the center of the street.

They say God works in mysterious ways. What he had in mind in this case is still a total mystery to me because it makes absolutely no sense at all. The very last relative I thought I'd see was also the very last relative I wanted to see. On my first day of looking for relatives, I'd found my father.

I don't know how we recognized each other. It had been six years. We'd both lost a tremendous amount of weight. When I'd last seen my father he'd weighed over 300 pounds. After his time in the camps he was probably under 150. But we did recognize each other. I have to remind you about my father. He never said much, and he wasn't a great father or husband. But you'd think that even a guy like that would jump for joy at seeing that his first-born son had survived. Instead he merely said, "I see you're still alive. I'm going to Paris."

I said, "Hello. I'm going to travel to the D.P. (displaced persons) camps to look for relatives. After that, I may try and go to my aunt in Dublin."

He said, "Go in good health."

That was it. That was our big reunion. He didn't ask about where I'd been, or invite me to go to Paris, or anything else. Just, "Go in good health."

I didn't find this out until years later, but almost immediately after liberation, my father had taken up with another woman. While I was searching for relatives all across Germany, deep down hoping to at least learn something of what had happened to my dear mother, he had simply replaced her. This hurts me deeply even to this day. I can only say that I am so very glad I didn't know this back then. How could he

91

throw out the memory of my dear mother so easily, so quickly, like yesterday's garbage? I am ever mindful of the wise words of Israel (or the black rabbi). I've clung to them all my days. I was a better husband. I am a better father.

I should explain a little about the D.P. camps, as I mentioned them a moment ago. D.P. camps were set up across Germany by the Americans and British as places where survivors could be nursed back to health, try to contact relatives, or at least try to figure out where to live. The Russians had similar camps.

I learned from the Red Cross that Russian occupied territory, which included all of Poland, was closed to all from the outside. Thus my search for relatives would need to be focused solely on D.P. camps within Allied occupied Germany.

To get to the major D.P. camps in Germany I'd need more than my new bicycle. That would be a major undertaking. On this day, my first day of searching, I'd found my father. You might say, "This was at least something." And I might respond, "A bucket of feces is something. A swarm of bees is something. A venomous snake is something. But are these things that help you? Are these things you want to carry around with you?" I met my father. He was still alive. I got back on my bicycle and peddled on back to Cham.

Chapter Seventeen

Searching for Relatives

I learned from the Red Cross, U.N.R.R.A. (United Nations Relief and Rehabilitation Administration), and Jewish Family Services about the locations of D.P. camps. I decided to start with Zeilsheim, a D.P. camp on the outskirts of Frankfurt. There were many D.P. camps located throughout Germany. I had to start somewhere, and I'd been told the one at Zeilsheim might be a good place to start. I packed my clothes in a small travel bag, all of which had been donated by local Germans.

I said goodbye to the nice German lady who had treated me so well during the few weeks I'd stayed in her home. She had more compassion and warmth in her little finger than my father would ever have. You might say, "Don't be so hard on your father. He'd lost his wife and children in the camps; of course he would become bitter."

If that were the case, what was his excuse before the Nazis came? The dear German lady had lost her husband and sons in the war. She still had a good heart. I lost my mother and siblings, really my entire childhood, and I wasn't going to be like my father. I promised myself that if I ever had a wife and children, I'd treat them the way my mother had treated me. I'd treat them the way the Israel Freidman, all the other wonderful American soldiers, and the kind German lady had treated me.

The combat elements of my liberators had moved on shortly after I'd settled in at Cham. However the support elements, of which Israel Friedman was a member, were still around. Israel and a group of soldiers walked me to Cham's little train station. When I was saying goodbye, Israel and the others repeated their offers to adopt me. Their generous offers were indeed tempting, but I felt a very strong desire to find my relatives. I thought that I may never see my mother and siblings again, but it would be good to at least find some relative.

I heard that although the war was over in Europe, a fair amount of soldiers would soon be leaving to fight the Japanese in the Pacific. I didn't know a thing about the war in the Pacific. I knew these brave men had already been through more than enough. It made me worry for the soldiers. My time in hell was over. It didn't seem fair. Why should they survive one hell just to be sent straight to another? Fortunately they never had to head off to the Pacific. Of course none of us knew this at the time.

Israel and I only spent the blink of an eye together. Even so he remains one of the most important and influential people I've ever encountered. From the moment we met, mere moments into my liberation, he took me under his wing. He was old enough to be my father, and with great sincerity offered to adopt me – to become my father. One of my deepest regrets in life is that I did not keep in touch with this wonderful man. Throughout my life I've often wondered how he was doing. Did he ever think of me? And of course I've wondered what life would have been like had I taken him up on his incredible offer to bring me into his family.

The Red Cross provided me with a D.P. card and told me I could use it to ride on trains and buses at no cost. I could also use it to get a little food at Red Cross and similar kitchens that had been set up at train and bus stations and D.P. camps throughout Germany. Lastly they gave me a couple wrapped sandwiches to take with me on the train. For six years food and generosity had been nearly nonexistent. So far, in my new life, both were in wonderful abundance.

I boarded a train at Cham. This was the second train ride in my life. It was on a nice passenger train with padded seats and big windows. It was marvelous compared to my first train ride inside the ghastly cattle car. The train was nearly full with a variety of travelers, including a fair number of survivors also heading to D.P. camps.

The train traveled slowly making many stops along the way. It took the better part of the day to make it to my first destination, Munich. Munich was by far the largest city I'd ever seen. I was totally flabbergasted by its size. What struck me most was the incredible amount of damage it had suffered under Allied bombing. As the train moved through bombed out neighborhoods, I noticed a kid my age picking through the rubble of a mostly demolished apartment building. He looked thin and dirty.

I suppose I could have hated him and felt happy at his condition. I'm no Gandhi or anything like that. However it's simply not in my nature to hate. Instead, I looked with pity on this young man. I wondered what it must have been like to hide in the basement of that building, fearing for your life, as bombs rained down from the sky. Had he lost family members in the war? Had he seen friends die?

At the main train station I switched trains to one heading to Frankfurt, which was another very large city. I was amazed by the size of these large cities. You have to remember before the camps I'd spent my entire life in a very tiny section of a fairly small town.

From the train station in Frankfurt I boarded a bus to the nearby town of Zeilsheim. Considering I was a fifteen year old boy, whose only experience with travel had been Nazi forced marches, I did pretty well navigating my way through these very busy train stations. I can't take too much credit, however. All along the way there were plenty of fellow survivors heading to D.P. camps. As in the camps, we looked out for one another. So, while I was travelling by myself, I was never truly alone.

The town of Zeilsheim had been converted into a D.P. camp. I was directed to a designated area where Red Cross, U.N.R.R.A., and Jewish Family Services representatives were available to help. Several of the representatives spoke Yiddish and Polish, both of which were my native languages. After my time in the Nazi camps, I spoke German fairly well. I'd also picked up a little Czech, Hungarian, and Rumanian from fellow prisoners. Here and there along life's way each of these languages has proven at least a little bit useful. It's a very big world out there. One can never have too many languages.

The representatives were very kind, offering food and a place to stay, as well as help relocating to relatives around the world. They also provided assistance in looking for relatives who survived the camps. This of course was my primary reason for being there. I showed them my D.P. card and told them, "My name is Bendet Fajner (my name would later become Ben Fainer); my mother's maiden name is Urman. I'm here for one reason and one reason only. I'm hoping to find Fajners or Urmans who survived."

There were large ledger books listing alphabetically the names of everyone who'd arrived at the D.P. camp. After checking the F's and U's, a woman told me, "I'm terribly sorry; there are no Fajners or Urmans in this camp."

She asked if I knew of any other names, perhaps the married names of some of my aunts. Sadly I couldn't remember. My mother had nine sisters. It had been six years since I'd been around my family, and I was just a kid back then. I did remember the married name of my mother's sister in Dublin, Ireland. The lady asked if I'd like to try and contact my aunt. I thanked her for her very kind offer. However I wasn't yet ready to give up on my search.

I stayed at the D.P. camp for a couple days resting and visiting with other survivors. There were thousands of survivors in the camp. We slept in make-shift housing set up in various buildings throughout the village. I stayed in a large warehouse building, which accommodated about 200-300 beds per floor. We talked to each other about our experiences, where we were held, and how we were liberated. It was nice, as no one was asking, "What's going to happen to us?" or any of the hundred variations of that worn out question asked so often in the camps and during the marches. I remember thinking, "This is how it should be. People should be able to live their lives without wondering if and how they might be killed tomorrow."

I asked the survivors if they'd run across any Fajners or Urmans at any of the camps. They hadn't. And each day I checked in with the people keeping the ledgers to see if any Fajners or Urmans had arrived. None had.

I left the camp more than a little disappointed. I think finding my father so easily, on the very first day of my search, had made me a little too hopeful. Deflated I took a bus from the camp back to the train station in Frankfurt.

I've learned since that not everyone moved on so quickly after visiting the D.P. camp at Zeilsheim. Many people stayed there quite a while. Over time the camp developed a strong community, with a theatre, cinema, music bands, and sports teams. A synagogue was established, which became very active in the Zionist movement. Schools were set up, including a training school for nurses. By February 1947 the camp community consisted of about 3,000 members. In November of 1948 the camp was closed.

It's a little difficult for me to understand how people could have stayed at a D.P. camp for so long. The whole time I was in the Nazi camps, I wanted so badly to get out in the world, so I could see and experience all of its wonders. The D.P. camps were as nice as the authorities could make them. People were free to stay or go as they pleased. However, in my mind, they were not the real world. They were a symbol of my old life, the life that had been so horribly and tragically mangled by the Nazis.

Please don't misunderstand me. I'm in no way criticizing the people who stayed. Many, many people had no place to go and not even a single living relative available to help them resettle. Some were ill or injured and needed medical care and time to recover. Some people had broken spirits. They needed a safe place to recover before they would be ready to move on. Staying in the D.P. camps made perfect sense for them.

My next destination was a D.P. camp set up at Bergen-Belsen, a former concentration camp liberated by the British. Unfortunately the train I needed to take from Frankfurt to Hanover was completely full. That did not stop me though. Along with five or six other people, I squeezed onto the stairs outside one of the passenger cars.

I spent the better part of the night riding on the stairs. I was able to doze off and on, thankfully without tumbling off the moving train. After one stop, as several passengers exited, a couple of the people with me were able to squeeze inside the car. This enabled me to move into their spot in the semi-protected alcove immediately outside the car door. This was a little safer than my previous place near the bottom of the steps.

By the time we reached Hanover, probably an hour or so before dawn, I was covered from head-to-toe with a thick coat of black soot. My face, hands, and clothes were totally black. This was the third train ride in my short life. It was much worse than the second and far, far better than the first. Inside the station I was able to wash up in the bathroom and change into a spare shirt I'd been given back at Cham.

I took a bus to the D.P. camp at Bergen-Belsen. Bergen-Belsen was the largest D.P. camp in Germany. It was known to have been a very tough Nazi camp, every bit as bad as those I'd lived through. Near the end the Germans had abandoned the camp leaving the prisoners locked up without food and water for about four days. When the British arrived on the scene, thousands of prisoners had died, their bodies strewn here and there across the entire the camp.

At first the British soldiers tried their best to gather and bury the dead by hand. There were simply far too many bodies to deal with. Fearing an epidemic, they reluctantly resorted to using bull dozers to push the piles and piles of bodies into mass graves. I've read descriptions of this sad and terrible process provided by the poor British soldiers who had to do this. I will not share these with you. You've already heard too much.

I arrived to a much better camp than what they'd found at liberation. All the bodies had been removed and buried in mass graves. After liberating the disease ridden concentration camp, as a health precaution, the British burned it to the ground. The D.P. camp was set up in a former German army camp that was near the actual concentration camp.

The British tried to re-name the D.P. camp, Hohne. Survivors insisted it retain the name Bergen-Belsen. Perhaps they feared a name change would make it easier for future generations to forget the horror they'd experienced there.

As with the D.P. camp at Zeilsheim, a thriving community sprang up at Bergen-Belsen. Originally it housed over 11,000 Jews. As life moved forward the camp averaged 20 weddings per day! A great number of Jewish residents of Bergen-Belsen immigrated to Israel; however many went to Canada and America. The last of the residents finally left the camp in August of 1951.

While I stayed there for only a very short time, everyone there could not have been more wonderful. As with the D.P. camp at Zeilsheim, none of my relatives had registered at the camp. I stayed for a couple days, again asking fellow survivors if they'd run across any Fajners or Urmans. Unfortunately none had.

Chapter Eighteen

Leaving Germany

There were D.P. camps all across Germany and other parts of previously Nazi occupied Europe. I'd been assured at both the D.P. camps I'd visited that there was no need to check any more camps. I'd registered with the Red Cross and other related agencies, and should any surviving relatives similarly register, the authorities would contact me at whatever forwarding address I provided. They told me I could go ahead and stay with my mother's sisters in London or Dublin. Therefore I decided there was no need for me to continue my search.

This made sense to me. I could get started with my new life, whatever that might be, with full confidence. I'd be notified if any relative registered with any of the D.P. related agencies. It wasn't an easy decision. I didn't want to be a quitter, to give up too easily. That isn't my nature. However I desperately wanted to start my new life.

I made my way by bus and train back to Cham. I decided to get things started on trying to live with my Aunt Ida in Dublin. I could have worked with the people at the D.P. camp at Bergen-Belsen, but I just felt more comfortable back in Cham. Also I figured if somehow things didn't work out to live in Dublin, I could see about living with Israel or one of the other soldiers.

Unfortunately Israel and his fellow soldiers had moved on a week after I'd left Cham. While Israel and I had said goodbye before I left Cham to search for relatives, I didn't know it was the last time I'd ever see him. He'd been so good to me. What a wonderful man! He was kind and had a great sense of humor. During our weeks together, just being around him had helped to heal my spirit more than anything. I wish I could have thanked him one last time for all he'd done for me.

I've recently been trying very hard to track down Israel's family. I'd love to learn more about him and tell his family members all he did for me. I'd love to talk with his children, to introduce myself as the adopted brother they almost had! Unfortunately I have not yet been able to locate Israel or his relatives. However, I have found a letter he sent home to his wife after his unit came upon Buchenwald. I will share some of this letter later in a section devoted to the liberation of Buchenwald.

The U.N.R.R.A., Red Cross, and Jewish Family Services representatives were fabulous. They helped the sick people with medicine and medical care. They also helped survivors contact relatives living in other countries. Without delay they were able to contact my mother's sister Ida in Dublin, Ireland. To my great relief, my Aunt Ida agreed to take me into her home.

When it was time to leave Cham, I said my goodbyes to all the people who'd been so kind. The wonderful soldiers who liberated me and treated me so kindly had already moved on. I carried with me a large envelope stuffed with odd scraps of paper. Each scrap contained a soldier's name, phone number, and home address. I took one long, final look at the wonderful little city of Cham. Then I climbed aboard the train bound for the German port at Hamburg.

I boarded a large German ship at the docks in Hamburg. It was basically a passenger ship, but also was used to ship all kinds of cargo. I'd never been on a boat: not even a little dingy. This was a pretty grand start. I don't remember the name of the ship. I wish I could. One of my daughters probably would have been able to find a photo of it on the Internet. You'll just need to take my word for it; this was a pretty big ship.

I quickly stored my very few belongings in my own little private room. It was the size of a small closet, with a small bed, and a sink.

Compared to the way I'd been living for the past six years, it was fantastic! I hurried back up to the deck and watched as the ship pulled away from the dock. My heart was divided. I was so very happy to be leaving Germany (for obvious reasons). However I was sad that I was leaving behind my hometown of Bedzin, Poland. I doubted I'd ever see it again. And of course I knew in my heart-of-hearts that I'd never see my dear mother and siblings again.

I stayed on deck watching the shore of Germany grow smaller and smaller, until finally I could see it no more. In an instant it was gone. I looked in every direction, and there was no land in sight. I was a sixteen year-old kid traveling across the open water. I was all alone. Like many things in life the feelings inside were a mixed bag. I was free, and I was heading toward a new life with family. But I was also all alone and leaving everything I'd ever known.

Believe it or not I was the only survivor aboard the ship. For the first time since I'd been taken from my home in Bedzin, I was not among fellow prisoners. Unless I told anyone, no one would know what I'd been through. It was quite an interesting feeling: not all great, but not all bad. It caused me to do a great deal of thinking. I was no longer 178873. I was no longer the son of a wonderful mother or an older brother to my dear siblings. I knew who I wasn't, but hadn't a clue as to who I was, or harder yet, who I'd become.

I passed the time on board chatting with some of my fellow passengers, especially those who could speak Yiddish or Polish. They knew from my tattoo that I'd come from the camps. They were curious, so I answered their questions. At that point I didn't mind talking about it, but more and more I took to wearing long sleeves. I didn't want to dwell on all those things. I needed to move forward.

Aunt Ida had made arrangements for me to visit another one of my mother's sisters in England on my way to Dublin. My Aunt Rosie lived in London. The ship arrived in Liverpool, and I took a series of buses and street cars to my aunt's home in London.

I can't describe how it felt to get a hug from my mother's sister. Life with Israel Freidman would have been great, I'm sure. But you know family is family. I'd never hug my mother again, but here was her sister.

I stayed with Aunt Rosie for four or five days. She cooked great Jewish meals! As I've said, my mother came from 14 generations of rabbis. In fact, if the Germans had never invaded Poland, I'm about

99.9% sure that I would have become a rabbi. It wasn't to be. A Yiddish proverb says, "To learn the whole Talmud is a great accomplishment; to learn one virtue is even greater." And of course my favorite virtue is hard work, but you've heard enough on that.

I hadn't had such food since living with my family in Bedzin. My mother was a very good cook, but because we were so poor she never had very much to work with. Aunt Rosie cooked many fine dishes, but I especially remember the fish, chicken soup, and lamb chops. They were wonderful!

She also took me all around London. I was amazed at how grand the city was. I saw Big Ben and the outside of Buckingham Palace. Aunt Rosie took me clothes shopping in some very nice London shops. I'd come a long way from our little apartment at Modrizejowska 77. I was stunned at the amount of damage the Germans had done to London. Even Buckingham Palace had been hit. I remember thinking how Hitler, one terrible man, could cause so much damage, to so many people, from so far away.

During the Blitz, which means lightning in German, the Luftwaffe bombed Great Britain and parts of Northern Ireland between September 7, 1940, and May 10, 1941. The Germans were trying to hinder British production and prepare for a planned invasion. Fortunately the bombing accomplished neither goal. Over one million houses were destroyed and 40,000 civilians were killed. Nearly half of these were killed in London, which at one point was bombed 57 nights in a row.

Aunt Rosie asked about the camps, so I told her a little, but held back on the horror. Then I told her that I hated to tell her, but from what I'd been told, my mother and siblings had been killed . I'd told Israel about this, but saying it to my aunt was different. This was my mother's sister, and I was breaking her heart. It was a very tough moment.

While people were curious about the camps, I could tell by their questions and the looks on their faces, that they didn't understand what had taken place. They didn't know all that we know today with all the books, movies, and the Internet. They'd heard a little about them in the news, but it was difficult for people to understand. How could they understand? They had nothing in their experience to prepare their minds to understand. I was there, and to this day I don't understand.

It was a very nice visit, but after three or four days it was time to catch a ship to Dublin. I said good bye to Aunt Rosie and made my way by street car and bus back to the docks at Liverpool.

I boarded an English ship, although I can't remember its name. I was assigned a little room, which I stayed in because the weather was bad. The sea was very rough. After a while a porter knocked on the door and said something in English that I couldn't understand. He tried again in a couple languages, but still I didn't understand. Then he said "eat" in Polish. I said, "Yes, please," also in Polish. He looked me over and must have thought I looked a little sea sick, so he said, "No. No eat."

Unfortunately I insisted. He brought in a little beef and lemonade and left shaking his head. I ate it, and in no time the voyage became a living hell. I felt so horrible. Honest to God, and I'm sure you'll find this hard to believe, but it was the worst thing I'd ever experienced. As you know that's saying quite a bit; I'm not exaggerating. For hours and hours I was totally miserable. I prayed to God for him to take me right there and then. Can you believe it? For over six years I'd prayed to God that he'd somehow keep me alive. But this was so bad that I truly wanted to die. I think God answers all of our prayers. Thankfully, in his wisdom, sometimes his answer is "No."

Chapter Nineteen

A New Life

Finally the hell was over. We arrived in the port of Dún Laoghaire (a.k.a. Dun Laoire). Aunt Ida, Aunt Laura, and her husband Abe were there to meet me. Ida and Laura were two of my mother's sisters. Barish and David, two of my mother's brothers, also lived in Dublin, but they were not able to greet me off the ship. All left Poland to settle in Dublin back in 1931. I can't help but wonder how my life might have been different had my mother joined them.

It was a fine greeting. They couldn't believe how healthy I looked considering all I'd been through. I explained to them how I'd been very sea sick on board and promised I'd look even better once the sickness passed.

We drove in Uncle Abe's brand new Buick. He was a wealthy man: the major supplier to the garment industry in Dublin. He liked new cars and usually traded in for a new one every year, sometimes twice in a single year. This was my first ride in a car, and it was a very nice way to start: plush leather seats, shiny chrome, and gorgeous blue paint you could see your reflection in. I said to myself, "I'm going to work my butt off, so someday I can buy a car like this!"

We drove to Aunt Ida's home at 18 Westfield Rd. in a southern suburb of Dublin. Near her house we passed an enormous white, stone church with two tall towers rising up on either side of its central entrance and steeple. It was quite impressive. I later learned it was Mount Argus. It was a Catholic Church set on the edge of Mount Argus Park, which was an expansive and beautiful park. I took it as a good sign that a wealthy Jewish family could safely live nearly across the street from a church. Again I wondered why our family hadn't gotten out of Germany with the rest of my mother's siblings.

That evening Aunt Ida hosted a large gathering of friends and family in my honor. After six years of being away from family, it was incredible to be surrounded by so many aunts, uncles, and cousins. I was still a bit queasy with sea sickness. I managed to eat some of the fine food, and this seemed to help. Everyone was very kind. They were curious about my time in the camps. I ended up telling and re-telling my story until things wrapped up sometime after eleven o'clock.

I could tell by the looks on their faces that no one understood the true horror of the camps. Their questions also showed a lack of under-standing, "Did they put on plays or musical concerts in the camps?" "How about movies, did they show any films?" This was not their fault. It was the norm for all those who'd not experienced the camps first-hand. During the war they'd heard rumors. At War's end they'd listened to radio reports from liberated camps. But no one could grasp what the Nazis had done. As the gathering came to a close, I felt utter-ly exhausted. The sea sickness had weakened me. Talking about the past six years had emptied me. I felt lost and hollow: a shell of a real person. As I drifted off to sleep I asked myself over and over, "Who am I? Who will I be?"

I shared a room with my cousin Bevin. He was quite interesting. While only just a little older than I, he was teaching economics and statistics at Trinity College! Trinity is the oldest, and perhaps finest, university in Ireland. He was a bit arrogant, but who wouldn't be? He was a true genius. Bevin eventually became a U.N. ambassador for France, which later on turned out to be a very lucky thing for my father.

Aunt Ida showed me all around Dublin for five or six days. After the week of touring Dublin, I started working at Aunt Ida's bakery. She owned the largest kosher bakery in Dublin, which made her a comfortably wealthy woman. After six years of starving and just bare-ly surviving on little bits of garbage, I spent every day surrounded by mountains of wonderful food. Since I was the owner's nephew, I got to eat anything I wanted. And so I did!

I like to say, "I was rolling in dough," but I only made about one British pound per week. One pound wasn't very much. It would cover a night out consisting of street car fare, a modest dinner, and a movie. It wasn't much, but Aunt Ida promised at some point she'd pay for me to attend Trinity College.

For the first few months all I did was grease the baking pans. Then I was promoted to work directly with the two bakers. They taught me how to make bread, bagels, and cakes. I also learned how to decorate cakes.

When I wasn't working, I was teaching myself how to speak and read English. I checked out Polish-to-English books from the library and studied in the evening. I'd read a word out loud and repeat it over and over again. As I mentioned my relatives were very observant Jews, so we couldn't do any type of work from sunset on Friday through sunset on Saturday. Technically practicing English is considered work. I wasn't worried about such rules, but I didn't wish to insult my aunt. I'd hide up in my room and get some good studying done during each Sabbath. I had to leave the door open because doing something like closing a door is considered work. The house was qui-et on those days, so I could hear anyone coming up the stairs or down the hall. If I heard someone coming, I'd hide the book and pretend to be praying.

I started going to a local dance club on Saturday evenings. It was a place where young people could listen to music and dance. One ev-ening I noticed a beautiful young lady across the room. I got up my courage and practiced the correct English words in my head. I crossed the room. Using my best, yet still broken English, I asked the young lady if she'd like to dance.

Without hesitation she replied, "No."

For about six months we repeated this brief exchange. I'd ask. She'd say no. Finally I decided I'd had enough. I needed to change my approach. I worked it out and practiced the English in my head. When I was ready I walked over and asked if she'd like to dance. As always she said no.

This time I didn't just leave it at that. I said, "Why won't you dance with me? I'm a good guy. I won't bite."

"I don't care. I don't want to dance with you," she answered.

"That was your last chance. I'm not going to ask you again," I said in a matter of fact tone and started to walk away.

She said, "Wait. Hold on; I'll dance with you."

I couldn't believe it! My heart nearly leapt out of my chest. But I didn't want to show it. My new approach seemed to be working, so I thought I'd keep it going. I said, "No. Now I don't want to dance ...but would you like to have a cup of coffee and a little bite to eat at the cafe?" There was a little cafe with tables in a quieter part of the dance club.

She agreed. I learned her name was Susan Christina O'Brien. But to me, she was Susie. She asked where I came from, I guess because of my accent. I told her that I was originally from Poland, but I lived with my aunt over on Westfield Rd. She noted this was a very nice part of town, so she knew I wasn't a bum. I told her I worked in my aunt's bakery. We talked and drank coffee for quite a while.

At the end of the evening I asked Susie if I could walk her home. She agreed, and as we walked I asked her why she'd been so tough on me over the past six months. Susie explained she just wasn't ready to get serious with anyone. I rolled my eyes and said, "Serious? I was asking you to dance, not get married! Are you going to be at the dance club next Saturday night?"

She said, "Maybe, maybe not."

She showed up the next Saturday night and every Saturday night to follow. We continued to dance and talk; over time we became quite close. We'd go out for dinner and dancing on Saturday nights. On Sundays we'd catch a movie together.

After about two or three months, while we were saying goodnight outside of Susie's home, I tried to give her a kiss. I'd been dreaming of kissing her since I'd first laid eyes on her. Every time I walked her home, I'd get all nervous inside trying my best to get the nerve to kiss her. Finally, on that night, I tried. My bold attempt was met by a firm slap on the face! "Ben Fainer, I'm not ready for anything like that!" my dear Susie told me.

Several weeks later, she was standing on one side of a low brick wall, and I was on the other. I put my hands down on top of the wall while reaching over to kiss her. Casanova I was not, as I'd put my

107

hand right down on a fresh pile of bird poop! I didn't get slapped, but rather Susie laughed with great delight!

A couple weeks later, Susie and I went out for dinner downtown. She was working at the Irish Hospital Sweepstakes making about three times my small weekly salary. That night she paid for dinner, and I made her promise to let me pay her back once I got paid the following week. After dinner, we peddled our bicycles back to her house. It wasn't yet close to midnight, which was when Susie needed to be home. Anytime close to midnight, I could count on her mother opening the door and yelling, "Susie, is that you out there?"

I took Susie's hand in mine. I looked her lovingly in the eyes, just as I'd seen in the movies. Then I reached over to give her a kiss. This time I did not get slapped in the face. Our lips met and my world changed! You could have knocked me over with a feather. My head spun and my heart nearly thumped out of my chest. The feeling I'd experienced at my liberation was incredible and wonderful beyond description. However it paled in comparison to how I felt when our lips first met!

So as they say, the third time is the charm! I knew she was the one for me, but I didn't think I was making enough money to get married. I asked my aunt for a raise so I could get my own apartment. I didn't tell her why, just that I wanted to be on my own. She didn't think it was necessary and told me to be patient and just keep living with her.

So I went to my Uncle Barish. He owned a very large garment factory. I told him I didn't think I wanted to make a career out of baking. I was interested in learning the clothing business and making it my trade. He agreed.

I explained this to Aunt Ida, and she was very gracious. I moved in with Uncle Barish at his home at 24 Hazelbrook Rd. I spent the first three or four months basting the pieces of clothing together. I sat atop a table and using white thread sewed the pieces into place. The tailors then sewed them together and removed the basting. Next I moved onto sewing using a single-thread machine.

After a year I asked Uncle Barish for a raise. I told him I wanted to move into my own apartment. He said that he wasn't ready to give me a raise. He told me to be patient. Undeterred I saved up my money and bought Susie a little diamond ring. I asked her to marry me, and to my delight she said yes. There was just one slight problem though. She was an Irish Catholic. I was a Jew. We didn't mind, but not everyone else around us felt the same way. Susie's parents were not happy at all. However, as she was totally committed, they decided to make the best of the circumstances. They felt it would be better to have a Jew as a son-in-law than to lose their daughter. Uncle Barish took the same practical approach.

Sadly my beloved Aunt Ida did not. She told me if I went through with this marriage, I would be dead to her. I explained that I was going to marry Susie, and nothing she said or did would change my mind. My Aunt Ida, my mother's sister, told me that in her eyes I was dead. At that point, I no longer existed.

This was a horrific blow to my heart. I was in love with a wonderful woman. What did it matter whether she was a Jew, Catholic, or whatever?

I was very grateful for all the help Aunt Ida and Uncle Barish had given me. However I am also the most independent S.O.B. you've ever laid your eyes on. I could have stayed in Dublin and eventually become very wealthy. But I never wanted to be dependent upon someone else. This was very important to me. Maybe growing up on my own in the camps had made me fiercely independent. Maybe I was just born that way. It's probably a little of both.

"Susie, I think we should move to America. I think there are more opportunities for people like us there," I explained later that day. To my amazement she thought it was a great idea!

I went to the United States Embassy and talked with a gentleman about my desire to move to America. He asked me if I had a trade and seemed satisfied that I was a tailor. Then he asked where I was born. I told him Poland.

"I'm sorry, but you can't move to the United States because you're a communist," he explained.

"Communist? What's a communist?" I really didn't know. Apparently the Cold War was starting up, and the U.S. had closed immigration to anyone from Soviet countries. The gentleman was kind, but there was simply nothing he could do. He did, however, recommend that I try the Canadian Attaché.

I went straight to the Canadian Attaché, and a man there said it would be no problem to immigrate to Canada. "How soon would you like to go," he asked.

I told him tomorrow would be just fine, but he said it would take a couple weeks to process the paperwork. Susie was happy, and we began getting ready for the move. I borrowed money from about a dozen of my friends, as well as some of their parents. I promised each I'd pay it back over time once we were on our feet in Canada. They knew I was an honest guy and a very hard worker. Their money was safe.

Next I went to give my Uncle Barish my two weeks notice. He couldn't believe it saying, "Bendet, why would you do this? Stay here. Be patient. You'll do very well here."

I thanked him for all his help, and told him my mind was set. Later, on his own, he went to see Susie. He told her he wanted me to stay. He said he'd give me a big raise, a car, and a house! This was all very generous, but our minds were made up. For better or worse we were starting off on our own. We were leaving all this behind and starting a new life.

Two weeks later our paperwork was completed. Susie and I were married in a Catholic church. Since I wasn't a Catholic the priest married us in the vestibule instead of before the altar. That very afternoon we boarded a ship bound for Liverpool. From Liverpool we boarded a nice English ship named the Samaria. We stayed in third class, which was in the bottom of the ship just like in the movie *The Titanic*. We didn't care third class or first class. We were young, and in love, and on our own. It was all very exciting!

We became friends with another young couple on board, Iris and Dennis. They were heading to Toronto. Susie and I were moving to Montreal. The first night at dinner the boat started to move up and down in the waves. I could feel the sea sickness coming on, but I tried and tried to fight it. Much to my embarrassment I actually threw up right there on the table. It was awful; I felt both very ill and very embarrassed.

Dennis took me out on deck where I continued to throw up until there was just nothing left to throw up. I asked Dennis to take me down to my room. Oddly he kept insisting that I follow him to the bar.

"Dennis, my friend, you don't understand. I'm sick as a horse. I need to go to bed – not to the bar!"

Dennis said he knew what he was doing; I should trust him. I knew from my horrible trip from Liverpool to Dublin that resting in bed hadn't made things any better, so I figured what the hell? We made our way to the bar, and Dennis ordered me two gin & tonics. I'd never had gin & tonic before, but I drank one and then the other. Sure enough Dennis was right. I started feeling better and was able to re-join the ladies.

Before moving forward to our life in Canada, I should mention something disturbing I've learned about Ireland. I hate to even mention it because I truly love the country and its people. After all I married its very best citizen.

Ireland remained neutral during World War II. They may have taken this strange position simply out of their deep anger at Great Britain, rather than of out of a liking for Nazi Germany. But even so, and this is the part I hate to mention, in response to news of Hitler's death, Eamon de Valera, the head of state in Ireland, visited the German Ambassador in Dublin. On behalf of Ireland he signed the official German Embassy book of condolence. I didn't know this until recently, and quite frankly, I don't know what to do with it. I'm confused and very disappointed.

Chapter Twenty

Canada

After seven days we arrived in Quebec. We said our goodbyes as Dennis and Iris boarded a train to Toronto. Susie and I found and boarded our train to Montreal. When we arrived at the train station in Montreal, I think I had only nine or ten dollars in my pocket. Immediately, right there in the station, we bought a newspaper and started looking for job openings.

We saw an opening for a cutter at a company called Crane Sportswear. "Susie, wait here for me. I'll go see about this job and be back as soon as I can," I told her.

I found Crane Sportswear down in the nearby garment district. I spoke with one of the owners named Rudy. He asked what I could do, and I said I could do everything. He said he needed a cutter and told me how much it paid. I can't remember the exact amount.

"Let me see what you can do," Rudy said, pointing to one of the very long cutting tables. I grabbed a scissors and got right to work. After a bit he said, "Not bad! I'll pay you double. Get to work and let me know if you have any questions."

"I need to ask you a favor," I said. "We just arrived by train this morning. My wife is waiting for me at the train station. Could I borrow $20 or $25, so we can find a little apartment? Then I can start to-morrow morning?"

He said, "You're kidding me? Your wife is waiting at the station? You seem like a good guy. Here's twenty-five bucks. I'll see you back here tomorrow morning."

So within a few hours of arriving in Montreal, with only ten bucks to my name, I got a job, and we found a little apartment!

Things were going very well for us in Montreal. However one day Rudy and his partner got into a big argument, and they decided to close their business. Rudy apologized to me and gave me one week's salary.

I quickly found another job in the garment district as a cutter for Meyzer, Miller, and Goodman: a manufacturer of made-to-measure suits. I was one of ten to fifteen cutters. The average cutter was able to knock out seven or eight suits a day. I was able to cut about ten to twelve at first, but quickly got up to 13 or 14. One day I even cut 15!

Then, to my great joy, my dear Susie became pregnant. On July 8th our first child, Michael, was born. What can I tell you? I was in seventh heaven! I didn't know much about being a father. But I knew for sure how not to be one. I promised myself to work as hard as I could to provide the best life possible for Susie and Michael.

I came home from work one evening about a week after Michael was born. To my horror I found Susie in great distress. She was crying and getting ready to stick her head in the gas oven to kill herself! She'd developed a serious infection in her breast from breast feeding. The pain was so unbearable that poor Susie just couldn't take it.

I called our doctor and asked him to come right away. He told me to take Susie to the hospital. I explained that I didn't have enough money to pay for a taxi. He said he didn't make house-calls, so I should try and borrow enough money for a taxi ride.

I didn't know what to do. I asked a neighbor if he knew of a good doctor. He told me to call Dr. Rubin and gave me his number. Thankfully Dr. Rubin arrived in no more than ten minutes. He checked over Susie and called for an ambulance to come right away.

Susie was taken to the Royal Victoria Hospital and immediately underwent emergency surgery. After a long while the surgeon came out and told me she was going to live. He said that had we waited even an hour longer, she probably wouldn't have made it.

I took Michael home leaving Susie to recuperate in the hospital. When I went to change his diaper, I saw that Michael had developed a similar infection on his left butt cheek. I took him to Jewish Hospital. The doctors explained that he'd need to stay there. So for two days I had to miss work. Each day I ran back and forth between the two hospitals. I didn't tell Susie about Michael because I didn't want her to worry.

After two days she was released. She was shocked when I told her about Michael. We went straight to see him, and thankfully he was doing much better. The next day he was ready to come home, so I went to pick him up. However they wouldn't let me take him home until I paid the bill in full. I was directed to a hospital administrator and was told I owed $1,000!

"My dear sir, I don't have $1,000. Isn't there some way I could pay a little out of every paycheck?"

The administrator told me no. I needed to come up with the money. Then I could take my son home. I couldn't believe it. I told him he'd just have to keep my son until I could earn the money, but it would take a long time. I told him that Michael was safe here. If there was no other way, this was my only option. The administrator told me I couldn't just leave him. I got up and started to walk out. The administrator changed his tune, and we negotiated a long-term payment plan.

It had been a very scary week. I'd nearly lost my dear Susie and our little baby. I was working as hard as I possibly could, but I just couldn't make enough to properly take care of my family. The next day I went to work and asked Rudy for a raise.

I was told I was being paid a fair wage for a cutter. If I wanted to make more, I'd need to stay there longer until a position as a tailor opened up. I argued that I was producing twice as much as any of the other cutters, so I should get paid twice as much. He wouldn't listen.

That night I told Susie that we should try things in Toronto. We'd kept in touch with Iris and Dennis, and things were working out well for them there. We packed up our things and boarded a train to Toronto.

We saw an opening for a cutter at a company called Beauty Form Lingerie. I said, "Susie, what's lingerie?" She laughed and told me it was underwear and nightgowns for women. I didn't care what it was. I just wanted a job.

I got the job, no problem. Over time I paid every penny back to the hospital in Montreal. Susie and I got to be very good friends with Steve Jeager, a Ukrainian, who was the cutting room boss. Life was pretty good. We had another child, Sharon. A little while longer we had our third child, Phil.

After about four years Steve told me he was going to move to California. He said people with our skills could earn a lot more money there. I told him that sounded fine, but that I couldn't get into the United States since I was born in Poland. Steve told me he'd heard that immigration laws had changed under the new American president. Eisenhower was president. He'd actually toured a concentration camp soon after its liberation, but I don't know if this had anything to do with the change in immigration laws.

In my heart I still wanted very much to go to America. It was the place everyone wanted to be. I'd seen all about it in all the movies I watched in Dublin. It was the homeland of the brave soldiers who fought their way across Europe to save me.

I checked with the United States Embassy, and to my delight they confirmed that Eisenhower had changed the rules. Since I was a Canadian citizen, and an Irish citizen before that, they no longer cared that I was born in what was now a communist country.

I talked with Susie about it, and she was thrilled. I gave my two weeks notice at work. While I was there a young girl named Maria came up to me in great distress. She said, "Benno," which is what she called me. "Mr. Goldberg keeps cheating us out of our pay. He hires people right off the train and promises them one amount to work. Then after you work, he cuts back the amount he promised. He does this all the time. It's not fair."

Beauty Form was a non-union shop owned by two brothers, Sidney and Phil Goldberg. Phil was a decent guy, but Sidney could be heartless. I told Maria I was leaving for America in two weeks, but I'd see what I could do.

I went down to the office of the International Ladies Garment Workers Union (I.L.G.W.U.) and asked how I could go about bringing the union to Beauty Form. The union leader, Sam Chrisman, told me that I needed to get the majority of workers to sign a union card, but I shouldn't get my hopes up. They'd been trying to get it unionized for years, but they had no luck.

Every night I met with small groups of workers and explained the benefits of the union. Within about ten days I was able to get 580 signatures out of about 582 workers! I returned to the I.L.G.W. office and told Sam I had a gift for him. I plopped down the signature cards before him on his desk.

"My God Ben, how in the world did you do this?"

"I don't mess around!"

Next I went to Beauty Form and walked up to Sidney Goldberg. I said, "Mr. Goldberg, I'm leaving to go to the U.S., but I have a little gift for you. The union is coming to Beauty Form. It's all set. There's nothing you can do about it."

He looked at me with disgust and said, "You're fired!"

"Mr. Goldberg. If you fire me, I'm going to raise my hand. See all those workers? They're watching us. If I raise my hand, we're going to walk out. Try and run your business without any workers."

He repeated, "You're fired!"

I raised my hand, and everyone stopped working. We all walked out. For days we walked the picket line on the sidewalk outside the factory. On the third day a Canadian Mounted Police, you know with the red jacket and sitting way up high on a horse, came up to me. He told me I needed to clear everyone off the sidewalk. I told him it was a free country. We weren't doing anything wrong, so we're not going anywhere.

After a couple more days the Goldbergs gave in. Phil Goldberg even asked me to stay and offered me a raise. It was too little, too late. Susie, our three children, and I were finally going to the United States of America!

Chapter Twenty-One

America

Times were really changing. Since Bedzin I'd ridden in trucks, trains, ships, and cars. We entered America in grand style. We flew in an airplane from Toronto to Chicago and then again from Chicago to St. Louis. I couldn't believe it! I stared out the window at the clouds and the world down below. I thought, "This is how things looked for the pilots flying the bombers over the factories near Buchenwald!" Everything looked so small. I was amazed any of the bombs actually hit the factories.

Our plans were to visit St. Louis briefly and then continue onto work with Steve, my old cutting room boss, in California. While we were living in Canada, my father had gotten himself into some legal trouble in France: something to do with smuggling. It may have been drugs, but honestly it could have been other things. I asked, but I never got a straight story out of him. I worked on his behalf with my cousin, Bevin, who was by then the French Ambassador to the United Nations. You'll recall he was my genius cousin I'd shared a room with for a brief time back in Dublin. He was able to get my father deported from France instead of facing charges for his crimes.

117

My father had married a woman named Hilda. They'd met in Germany soon after liberation. You'll recall that while I was travelling all across Germany searching for relatives, hoping against hope somehow my mother and siblings had survived, he went right out and found a woman to replace my mother. What kind of man does this? No wonder he hadn't asked me to come with him to Paris. I was a leftover from a life he'd already buried. He'd already turned the page.

After living together in Germany for a while, they'd moved to Paris. There he'd gotten into his trouble and then resettled in St. Louis. I'd heard he'd mellowed a bit, so I thought it might be good for Susie and the children to meet my father. I know you probably think I was stupid or crazy. I'm an optimist to a fault. And I'm a little old fashioned. Family is family. A father should meet his son's wife. Children should meet their grandfather.

My father and Hilda picked us up from the airport. He was a tailor during the day, and as I soon learned, still a drunk at night. He was a little older but not a bit nicer. For some reason he wanted us to settle in St. Louis. Perhaps he thought it would be handy to have me around to take care of him when he got old. I'm an optimist, but I'm not stupid. I knew he didn't want me around simply to get to know me and catch up on some father-son bonding!

I asked him if he'd received any letters from my friend Steve, as I'd given him my father's address as a good place to contact us when we arrived in the States. He said that he'd not received any letters. Later I learned that he'd indeed sent information to my father's home. My father had simply thrown them away. Like I said, he wanted us to stay.

One of my children had a little stomach trouble while we were staying at my father's house. Unfortunately he had an accident and soiled one of my father's chairs. My father became irate yelling that he'd paid $300 for the chair, and now it was ruined. Susie and I tried to clean it, but the stain still showed. My father insisted we pay him for the chair, which I did over time. I later mentioned this incident to a mutual friend. He informed me that my father had not paid $300 for the chair. The friend had been with my father when he bought the chair at an estate sale for $25. That was the type of man I had for a father.

We'd been in St. Louis for several days, when I decided to visit the local I.L.G.W.U. office to see if they knew anything about the company Steve worked for in California. I chatted with the union representative and told him I was an experienced cutter. At that very second the phone on his desk rang. It was a call from a man named Albert Barad. He owned a large clothing operation and was looking for an experienced cutter!

I told the union representative that I wasn't interested in staying in St. Louis; I was going to California. He told me that I might not like California. He said it was a very busy place, with a lot of traffic, and it was very expensive to live there. "St. Louis is a very nice place to work and raise a family. You should go talk with Mr. Barad about this job," he urged.

So I went to see Mr. Barad at his office down in the garment district, which is located downtown along Washington Avenue. I was very impressed with him and his business. For numerous reasons Susie and I were ready to move out of my father's house. However we hadn't received any letters from Steve about jobs in California. I didn't know yet that my father had thrown them away. So I agreed to start working for Mr. Barad but only on a temporary basis. Mr. Barad even arranged for one of his employees to drive me back to my father's house.

I began working at Barad Lingerie the very next day. We moved into a little apartment on Maple Avenue. I wasn't making great money, but we were getting by. After about six months we moved again to another apartment at Westminster and Holly Mount. It wasn't very nice, and the neighborhood was a little rough. After we lived there for about six months, I got a great surprise when my friend Steve showed up unannounced from California.

"Ben," Steve asked, "what's the matter with you? I thought you were dead! I've been calling your father's house and sending telegrams. I got very worried; I flew out here to make sure you are okay. Why haven't you answered me?"

I couldn't believe my father had done this. Steve said he had a great job lined up for me. I told him how sorry I was, but that we'd already settled into life in St. Louis. Steve was a little disappointed, but he was relieved to find that I was alright. He stayed for two or three days before flying back to California.

One morning, as Mr. Barad walked by my cutting table, I said, "Excuse me Mr. Barad. Is it possible that I could speak to you in private?"

"Sure Boy. Come along with me now, and tell me what's on your mind." Mr. Barad always called me "Boy." He meant it in a kind way.

"Mr. Barad, I've worked here for little over a year. My wife is very disappointed with life in America. We live in a bad neighborhood. The teenagers hang out and throw beer bottles against the walls. We don't even have money to buy furniture. My children sleep on the floor. Our little one sleeps in a drawer. Would it be possible to borrow some money from you so we could buy a little house someplace nice like University City? I will pay it back out of every paycheck. I could also take on a second job to pay it back faster."

Without hesitation, Mr. Barad told me, "No problem. How much do you need?"

I'd already looked into buying a little house from a friend of mine who worked at Sara Lee. He had a house at 6839 Julian in University City. He was asking $15,500, and I'd been able to talk him down to $14,200. "Mr. Barad, I need $4,000 or $5,000 for the down payment."

Mr. Barad smiled and picked up the phone. He got Adel Bronze, the office manager, on the phone. "Adel, please make a check out to Ben Fainer in the amount of $5,000. Have it ready for him to pick up at the end of the day."

I almost had a heart attack! Susie was so excited. We bought the house with the down payment and a Federal loan. Then we took on a bit of debt to buy some proper furniture. We went to Beidermans Furniture Store and bought bunk beds, a nice bed for our bedroom, and a little kitchen table with chairs. We were finally able to live like proper human beings. We were very, very happy.

Mr. Barad had two sons working with him, Lenny and Mel. They were wonderful people. Mr. Barad treated me like a son. I started making payments to him right away. Lenny called one evening and said, "Ben, you're a great guy. You're doing a fine job. I have an opportunity for you to make a little extra money. I have a friend over at Fancy Free. They really need a cutter. They specialize in maternity wear, so they don't compete with us. They're flexible with the hours, so you could do it whenever it works out for you, as long as it doesn't interfere with your work here."

I started right away at Fancy Free working every evening once I finished up work at Barad's. After a little while I took on an additional part-time job with a clothing company called Two Brothers. I worked for the brothers, Marc and Lenny Rosenfeld. There I would cut napkins and table cloths, which they sold through their mail order business.

Between the three jobs I worked an average of about 80 hours a week. I still managed to spend time with Susie and the kids every spare minute of every day. People would say, "Ben, you work so hard. Don't you ever get tired?" I honestly rarely get tired.

Getting tired in the camps could get you killed. Maybe I just got used to working hard and getting by on very little sleep. Maybe it's my nature. I know one thing; I was motivated. I wanted to be a good husband and a good father. To do this I had to work hard to provide for them. But I also needed to find the energy to be a good husband and father when I got home. It was very important to me to be a good husband and father. I often thought of what Israel and the rabbi had told me back in Cham. I had to work hard to be the person I wanted to be. Otherwise I might follow the bad example of my own father.

After a few years I was promoted to head cutter at Barad's. I'd get up early and head downtown. After a quick breakfast at Hollings Restaurant, I'd open up at Barad's at about 7:30. As head cutter, aside from the Barad's themselves, I was the only one entrusted with keys.

Life was great! Susie and I had four more children in St. Louis bringing our total to seven. Each time she was ready to deliver, I'd take some time off from work. While she was in the hospital, I'd take over the care of the children and home. I'd wake the kids, feed them, and get them off to school.

Every so often, whenever Mel Barad was ready to buy a new station wagon for his family, I'd buy his old one. He took very good care of his cars, and he always gave me a pretty good deal on the price. This worked out very well for us. Whenever I had a light work day on the weekend, Susie and I would pack up the kids in the station wagon and head out to explore the area. We'd enjoy a special family day visiting all kinds of local attractions, such as the St. Louis Zoo or the Jesse James Museum.

Once I was making enough, I was able to take off a whole week. We'd enjoy a family vacation to the mountains of Tennessee or the beaches of Florida. It was great fun! I loved spending so much time with Susie and the children.

Life in St. Louis was working out just fine. Work and family kept me so busy, often days would pass without a single thought of the camps crossing my mind. People had moved on from the war. If any-one knew I'd been in the camps, they didn't seem to care. That was just the way I liked it. I didn't want to be Ben Fainer, the Holocaust survivor. I just wanted to be known as a good father, a good husband, and a good tailor.

Somehow a guy at the local I.L.G.W. office found out that I'd been in Buchenwald. One day he said, "Ben, you really need to meet Felix Moskovich, the manager at Carlee Clothing. He was at Buchen-wald."

Barads Clothing was on the second floor of 1520 Washington Avenue. Carlee was on the third floor of the same building. I got busy with other things and more or less forgot about this. However one day it popped into my mind, and I decided to stop in to meet Felix.

I met Felix at Carlee, and we talked for a little while in his private office. We were both startled to learn that we'd been at Buchenwald at the same time. Even more shocking, we'd both lived in Block 15! What are the chances that two guys from horrible Block 15, living next to the crematorium sheds, would end up working one floor apart in the same building in St. Louis, Missouri?

Neither of us remembered the other from the camp. The barracks held a couple hundred guys, so that's not surprising. Also we didn't look like normal people in Buchenwald. We were walking skeletons wrapped in a thin layer of pale skin. I may have seen Felix a thousand times in Block 15. No one in the camps looked anything like normal people.

Felix and I became lifelong friends. We kept in touch when he moved to Atlanta, and we even visited him there. Felix and I enjoyed chatting together over drinks, but we didn't talk about the camps. What was there to talk about? He knew what I knew. I knew what he knew. I've been trying to reach him recently, but I'm not having any luck. I'd like to see how he's doing. He's a few years older than I am, so I pray he's still around.

Chapter Twenty-Two

Working for Others and for Myself

I worked with a fine gentleman at Barads, Al Grandlich. Al was the production manager in charge of the factory where the items I cut were finished. At a certain point Al had a disagreement with Albert Barad and decided to leave. He went to work for Smoeller Brothers, a Chicago based ladies apparel company. Al was in charge of their factory in Herron, IL. One day Al called me and asked if I'd be interested in working as head cutter for Smoeller Brothers cutting operation, which was in Frankfort, IL, not far from their factory in Herron.

Initially I told Al that I didn't think I'd be interested. I'd worked for the Barads for nearly 20 years, and they'd been very good to me. But he was persistent and invited Susie and me to have a nice dinner with him and his wife. At dinner Al explained that Smoeller Brothers had been through numerous head cutters in the past year. It was a good company, but the workers at the West Frankfort operation were very difficult. They were somewhat clannish: not trusting anyone from outside the area. Al had seen me working with cutters at Barads. He knew I was a fine cutter and worked very well with people.

Out of loyalty I was hesitant to leave Barad's. However I'd been having difficulty working with a recently hired vice president. She

123

wanted to control everything, even things she knew very little about. She'd come out on the cutting room floor and try to boss everyone around. I get along with everyone. I tried everything but couldn't figure out a way to work with her. So this lady pecked away a little chink in my loyalty to the Bards. When Al said he'd triple whatever the Barads were paying, what could I do? Loyalty to the Barads is one thing, but I had to provide for my family.

I gave notice with the Barads, which was very difficult. They couldn't believe it, but they wouldn't triple my pay. Nor would they fire their difficult vice president.

I took the job of head cutter with Smoeller Brothers. We moved to Marion, IL and had a very nice home built. Head cutter was considered a management position. Smoeller Brothers was a union shop, so for the first time in my life I had to quit the union.

Al had warned me about the workers being difficult with outsiders, so I spent the first two weeks doing nothing but watching and politely asking questions. I was in charge of 57 women shop workers and six or seven male cutters. Once I had everyone sized up, I began carefully making suggestions. I'd approach someone very quietly, so I wouldn't draw attention and make them feel embarrassed.

I'd say something like, "I've noticed that you're doing such and such this way. I'd like to make just a small suggestion that might improve things quite a bit. Would you try doing it this way for just a little bit and see how it works? If it doesn't, you can go back to your way of doing it."

I repeated this here and there really trying to be respectful and gentle. It didn't work. They just kept doing things their own way. So I called them all into the lunch room. I told them, "I have a wife and seven children. I need this job. How badly do you need this job? You've chased out head cutter after head cutter, but let me tell you, I'm not going anywhere.

"I'm not telling you to do things differently just to boss you around. I've been in this business since I was 17 years old. I've been a cutter over at Barad's for the past 20 years. I know how to do this. Trust me and do as I say, and we'll make the bosses at Smoeller Brothers very happy with us. We might be able to earn a raise by doing a good job on our own without the union's help."

Things didn't improve. In fact one day I was talking with a cutter about a better way of doing something, and I grabbed the cutting machine to show him the technique. The cutter complained to the union saying I was doing union protected work.

The union rep showed up for a visit. We knew each other from my years in St. Louis. He told me the complaint, and I explained what had taken place. He assured me what I did was just fine. Later another complaint was filed, and again the rep told me what I was doing was okay.

We were getting some big orders, so I asked if anyone would like to earn some over-time. Only about two signed up. I asked again saying that I'd provide dinner and soda, and this time about 30 signed up. One of the office staff pulled me aside and asked, "How are you going to pay for all this?"

I told her I was going to use the money the Smoeller Brothers made from the employee vending machines. She told me I couldn't do that; the money was supposed to be sent to their headquarters in Chicago.

I told her I was doing only what was in the Smoellers' best interest. I was the head cutter. I was spending a little on the employees, so we could handle the big orders. It wasn't like I was spending a great deal of money or off buying my wife clothes.

After I'd done this for a while, sure enough, I got a call from an accountant at Smoellers in Chicago. He asked why they weren't receiving any vending machine money from us. I explained how I was using it, and he told me, "Great job. We're very pleased with how things are going down there. Keep up the great work."

It took me about a year to turn matters around at the cutting operation in West Frankfort. It was a challenge but also a great learning experience. Sadly, after about two years, business wasn't going so well for Smoeller Brothers. There was a lot of talk about needing to close down the operations in Herron and West Frankfort. My friend Al told me he was leaving; I should consider doing the same.

We sold the house and moved back to Missouri. We lived in a town-house in Creve Coeur, which is a nice suburb of St. Louis, while waiting for our new home to be completed. However while shopping for furniture, I slipped on ice and broke my right arm. I'm right handed, so this kept me out of work for about six months.

Once it healed I started working as a cutter at Groves: a non-union shop on Manchester Road. Groves specialized in plaids which can be a little tricky to work with. The lines within the plaid pattern need to line up very precisely along the seams. It's work that is best left only to very experienced cutters.

I wasn't making very much money there, but I needed the job because I'd been out of work with the injury. One day I noticed that the spreader had been careless. The spreader's job was to roll out the cloth and make sure it's all lined up properly. He hadn't double-checked the stack of cloth to make sure the plaids would all line up. I said, "Hey, you didn't double check. If I had cut these, they would have all been ruined."

I brought this to the attention of the owners. I said, "I just saved you about $25,000 in ruined material." I explained what had nearly happened and asked for a raise. They said no. I'd needed to work there longer before I could get a raise.

Then I found an ad for a cutter at Angelica Uniforms. They were a union shop specializing in lab coats and surgical smocks. I got the job, which paid a fair wage. It was a solid company, and I enjoyed it quite a bit. However I'd always thought it would be better to own my own business. So after I worked at Angelica for about six or seven years, I started my own company called, "Scrubs by Doc."

One day I was chatting with my neighbor over a couple beers. He was an engineer from Australia working for Sigma Chemical in St. Louis. He happened to ask me what I did, and I explained about my uniform business.

He said, "How'd you like to talk with the buyer at Sigma?"

Of course I said I'd love to. He set up an appointment, and I met with a buyer named Mike Clemmy. I showed him some samples, and we discussed what he was paying for each item. I was able to beat the prices Sigma was paying, so we signed a contract making me the exclusive supplier of lab coats and similar items. Mike said they needed to supply items to Sigma's operations world-wide, which would probably mean about 1,200 lab coats a month!

Things were really going well, so I expanded to include pants and jackets. Next I took out a loan and opened my own retail store in a quaint little area of the suburbs called Hog Hollow. I named the store "The Rag Patch."

Unfortunately the store didn't do very well. After about five years I fell behind on my payments. I got a visit from a gentleman from Community Federal Bank which held my business loan. He asked me why I wasn't making payments, and I explained that the business wasn't doing well; there just wasn't enough money.

He told me I'd need to start making payments, or the bank would take away my home. I told him, "I don't have the money. It's just not there. I don't have a money tree. I will pay you whatever I can as soon as things get better. If that's not okay, then I'll have to call my friend, Mr. Armbruster. I don't think he will want you to take my home."

I knew Mr. Armbruster was the head of Community Federal, but I didn't know him from Adam! Maybe my bluff worked, or maybe the loan officer decided the bank really didn't want to take my home. Whatever the case, I was very relieved. Losing my home would have been an enormous personal failure. How could I have faced my dear Susie? Fortunately I was able to sell the store and begin making payments soon after.

I continued to sell uniforms with Sigma as my largest customer. Rather than selling my other lines through my own store, I decided to try and sell to a large retail chain. I was able to get a meeting with a buyer at a large chain, Famous & Barr. I brought some of my samples. Famous was buying polyester pants from a place in New York for $3.75 a pair and selling them in their stores for about $9.75. I offered to produce them for 40 to 50 cents less.

The buyer agreed and made an initial order of 20,000 pants! He wanted them in 30 days! I was happy, but this was a little crazy. I was small potatoes compared to most of the suppliers dealing with Famous & Barr. I wasn't set up to handle that kind of volume.

I had a friend, Murray Goldberg, who used to buy material odds and ends from the Barads. He'd buy them at a huge discount and store them in a large warehouse. I negotiated to purchase enough material for the 20,000 pants, but I didn't have the money to pay for it up front. Since Murray knew I was a good guy, he agreed to let me pay him after Famous had paid me. Somehow I pulled it off. I was able to produce and deliver 20,000 pants within 30 days!

The next order came in for 15,000, and they just kept coming! I was able to pay off all my debt. I asked Susie, now that we were debt free, if she thought I should continue with my own business or go back to working for others. She told me to keep going with my business.

It was the late '70s or maybe early 80's. I had Sigma and Famous Barr as my main clients and even expanded into ladies golf-wear, which I sold through golf clubs and stores. We were doing pretty well. Susie and I started taking nice trips. We went on cruises to exotic places like St. Thomas. It was wonderful. I was finally seeing more and more of the incredible world I'd dreamed of seeing while in the camps. I'd come a long way from that small apartment in Bedzin, Poland!

All was great, but then my dear Susie started not feeling well.

Chapter Twenty-Three

Susie

Before I get to that, I forgot to tell you about a great thing Susie encouraged me to do. This happened just a little before I started my own business. I throw it in here since I'm talking a little bit about my dear Susie.

One night Susie and I returned home after an evening out at a veteran's hall just over in Illinois. Susie made me a little Scotch, gently touched my arm, and said, "My Benny Dear, I think you should call your family in Dublin. They're not getting any younger. Maybe it's time to make peace. Please do this favor for me."

"Don't ask me to do this. I don't want to open that can of worms," I replied. But, of course, I could never say no to my dear Susie. She knew this and even had the phone number handy. I was nervous. My heart was pounding and my hands were shaking. I dialed the number. It rang and rang. Finally a voice answered. I knew in an instant it was my mother's brother Barish.

"Uncle Barish, this is your nephew Ben, I mean Bendet."

I didn't know if he'd hang up or what. He didn't. Immediately he said, "Oh be Jesus!" This might seem like an odd thing for a Polish

Jew to say, but you have to remember he'd lived in Dublin since the 1930s.

"Ben, when are you coming home?"

"Uncle Barish, I'm an American. This is my home."

"How are you? It's so good to hear from you after all these years!"

"Susie and I are doing great! We have seven children. We're really quite happy. We'd like to come visit our families in Dublin this Christmas. I want to let bygones be bygones. I would love to visit everyone and anyone who is willing to see us."

As it turned out Bevin's son was set to be married during our planned visit to Dublin. Bevin is my Aunt Ida's son (the young genius I shared a room with while I lived with her in Dublin).

Susie and I arrived at a pre-wedding party. I was nervous but also very excited. All my uncles, aunts, and cousins were there. After introducing Susie to everyone who'd greeted us in the entrance hall, my Uncle Barish took me aside and asked if I'd like to introduce Susie to Aunt Ida.

I took Susie by the arm and we followed Uncle Barish down a hallway and into a little sitting room. The last time I'd seen my Aunt Ida, she'd told me, "If you marry this gentile, you will be dead to me. You will be no more."

Aunt Ida hugged and kissed me. She broke into tears and told us how terribly sorry she was. Aunt Ida hugged and kissed Susie and said she was very happy to have her part of the family.

As it turns out, Ida had a son by a second marriage. That son grew up and became engaged to an Irish Catholic girl. Ida, when faced with this dilemma for a second time, chose to accept the mixed marriage. Over the years she'd grown to love her son's wife and regret how she'd dealt with Susie and me.

The fence had been mended. After that we kept in touch. Susie and I traveled to visit all our relatives in Dublin several more times. This was a great joy to my heart. I owe it all to my dear, dear Susie!

She was the love of my life. After the horror of my childhood, God blessed me a million times over by giving me such a wonderful wife. We shared a story-book life, including seven wonderful children: Michael, Sharon, Phil, Sandy, Janice, Cynthia, and Gary. Susie was the best mother a child could ever wish to have. She loved and cared for each and every one of our seven children without ceasing.

Being able to take Susie on nice cruises was one of the greatest joys to my heart. In 1995 we took a wonderful cruise to St. Thomas. When we returned she told me she wasn't feeling very well and had some pains in her stomach. We went to the doctor thinking maybe she'd picked up a little stomach flu or something on the trip. We were devastated to learn that she had an aggressive form of cancer. They've made great progress in treating many forms of cancer. Unfortunately the type Susie had was not one of them.

I've told you of the horrors I experienced in the camps. As I've said, I feel as if I have to. But forgive me if I don't go into detail about losing my dear Susie. This is all I will say. I had the most wonderful mother: the queen of all mothers. I lost her to Hitler. I had the most wonderful friend and wife. I lost her to cancer. It was the most horrible experience of my life.

Chapter Twenty-Four

A Very Persistent Woman

One day I got a phone call from a woman named Marci Rosenberg. She told me she was working with the Shoah Foundation collecting video interviews of Holocaust survivors. She wanted to tape my interview.

I told her I didn't want to talk about it. I'd been through it. I'd put it behind: end of story. The woman ignored this and went on to make her case. She told me it was very important. People are starting to deny it ever happened. The video would be kept with others at every Holocaust museum in the country. It would help to show future generations it happened. As you might know by now, I'm a little stubborn. I thanked her for calling, but I insisted that I wasn't interested.

A few weeks later I heard my doorbell ring. I opened the door and saw an attractive woman at my doorstep. She reached out her hand and introduced herself as Marci Rosenberg. I invited her in, and again she tried to convince me to be interviewed for the Shoah Foundation. Once more I declined.

After a few years I moved to Florida. This is when I became friends with the rabbi and had my Bar Mitzvah. And of course that's when my friendship with one of my liberators, Norris Nims, began.

Having lived in northern climates my entire life, I enjoyed my time in Florida. However I missed my family, so I returned to St. Louis along with my beloved Golden Retriever, J.T. The two of us moved in with my daughter Janice and her family for a while before we eventually settled into a nearby apartment.

In no time Marci Rosenberg once again showed up on my doorstep. She is a very persistent lady. I said, "My dear Miss Rosenberg...."

She cut me off and insisted I call her Marci.

"Marci. I don't know what to do with you. You might as well whistle a gig to a milestone. I don't know if I should throw a bucket of cold water on you and tell you to go away, or give up and invite you in for coffee!"

"Mr. Fainer...."

I cut her off and insisted she call me Ben.

"Ben. I'd really prefer you invite me in for coffee, if it's not too much trouble."

I invited her in. I made a little coffee. She started right in where she'd left off during her previous two attempts. She's really quite something. I mean that in a very good way. Marci is attractive, charming, intelligent, and very persistent. What struck me most of all was her passion. She's intensely dedicated to preserving the stories of Holocaust survivors. Marci strongly believes it is incredibly important. She is doing everything in her power to make sure people never forget and never allow it to happen again.

Her passion was infectious. After all those years and years of keeping silent, this wonderful young lady changed my heart and mind. Reluctantly I agreed to tell my story.

After making the arrangements, she arrived with a camera crew at my apartment. I don't think I slept a wink the night before. I was nervous. I was scared about opening up the past. I had pushed the horror out of my mind. It hadn't been easy, but I'd lived many very good years that way. I didn't know how it would feel to relive it all. I was most afraid of talking about my dear mother. I'm a proud man. I didn't want to cry in front of Marci and the camera crew.

Once we got started it all began to spill out. When I mentioned my mother, my eyes got wet and my voice maybe cracked a little bit. But everything was okay. The more I said, the easier it got. We'd take breaks every so often when they needed to change a tape, or someone needed to use the bathroom. The whole thing lasted about five or six hours. It wasn't easy by any means. Nor was it therapeutic. I didn't feel cleansed or released from the scars of my past. But I was no longer afraid of them. I began to understand that they're a part of me.

Marci hugged and thanked me for sharing my story. I hugged her back and thanked her for helping me do it. After she left I called my dear friend Norris,

"Norris Baby," that's what I called him all the time, "I did it. They set up a camera and a microphone, and I told them everything. It wasn't so bad. I did the right thing."

Norris told me he was very proud of me. Hearing that from a great man like Norris was the highest praise I'd ever received. I cherish his compliment as if I'd been given the Medal of Honor!

Marci and the crew set up another video interview with several of my children. I'd never talked with them about what I'd been through. My dear Susie had known a little. She'd told them all she knew. Other than that, they only knew what they'd learned about the Holocaust at school and on TV.

Marci wasn't finished with me. She was on the board of the St. Louis Holocaust Museum and Learning Center. She called me one day and asked if I would start giving talks to groups visiting the museum.

I said, "My dear lady, I'm not an educated man. I barely went to school in Poland. I've had to teach myself to speak, read, and write in English. I have a thick Polish accent. I'm a tailor, not a public speaker. Forgive me for saying this, but I'm afraid you must be out of your mind."

Marci stressed the importance of survivors speaking directly to people. "They can read it in a book or see it on TV, and that's good. But if they hear it directly from you, in flesh and blood, right in front of them, it will change their lives. Then when they see the horrible photos, they won't just see nameless victims. They will see you."

I gave my first talk to a church group of about 40 people. Of course I didn't sleep the night before, and I was so nervous, but forgive me for saying, I felt like I would dodo in my pants. My eyes became wet and my voice cracked when I talked about my dear mother, but I made it through it. The people were wonderful. Many came up afterward and shook my hand or gave me hugs.

Marci told me I did a great job. I started giving talks at the museum on a regular basis. Then she called me one day with a very interesting invitation.

"Ben, the Holocaust Museum in Washington D.C. is holding a very special event honoring World War II veterans who liberated Nazi camps. There's a very generous businessman in St. Louis, a great supporter of our museum, named Michael Staenberg. He's offered to pay for several of us from the museum to attend. We've all talked it over, and we'd very much like you to join us."

I was totally flabbergasted. You know of my love for the brave American soldiers who liberated us. I told her, "I would be honored to go. I'd even walk there if I had to."

Marci, two other ladies from the museum, and I flew to Washington D.C. Mr. Staenberg put us up in The Mandarin Oriental Hotel: the fanciest hotel in the whole city. The first evening we attended a very nice welcome reception, where I was able to meet and thank many liberators. I was in seventh heaven!

The next morning we attended a ceremony at the Holocaust Museum. I wanted very much to see a section I'd read about showing the rise of Hitler and how he'd carefully set the stage for the Holocaust. I didn't want to see any other part of the museum. I'd lived it. Seeing it actually happen was enough.

Once inside the museum, I accidently went through a doorway that led me straight into an area about Buchenwald. I saw what I didn't want to see. It was too much. I needed to get outside in the sunlight. I needed to breathe fresh air. Immediately I apologized to Marci and the ladies. I told them I'd go have some coffee and meet up with them after they'd toured the museum.

It's an incredible museum, as is our museum in St. Louis. If you weren't in the Holocaust, I beg you to visit them. Go hear a survivor tell his or her story while we're still around. The Germans weren't any different than any of us. If it happened to a modern 20th Century European country, it could happen anywhere. It could happen here. You owe it to your children and grandchildren to hear a survivor while you still can. You must make sure it is not forgotten.

Next we attended an incredible ceremony in the rotunda in the Nation's Capitol. I was honored to be there, and I even met and spoke with the general in charge of the Israeli Air Force.

That evening we attended a grand dinner in honor of the liberators and survivors. U.S. Attorney General, Eric Holder, Jr., gave a powerful speech, as did generals and many others. It was in a gigantic ballroom with waiters serving wonderful meals to over 1,200 guests. I had sea bass, which was out of this world! I just kept looking around, and thinking about being at such a fancy dinner, and saying to myself, "My God Ben Fainer, you've come a long way from carrying buckets of water in Bedzin, Poland!"

Chapter Twenty-Five

My Liberators – Our Liberation in Cham

I have a great love for American soldiers. I'm a proud American. As a country we don't always do everything right, but at our core we have a big heart. We're always trying to help people.

The guys who liberated me were heroes. They'd been through their own hell on their way to saving us. As you know the World War II soldiers don't talk about it much. They saw and had to do a lot of things people who weren't there could never imagine. I understand that. Liberators and survivors have a lot in common. Even though we came from very different places, we both survived our own kinds of hell. Then we had to put it all behind and start new lives. We had to move on.

As you know, I became great friends with one of my liberators, Norris Nims. He used to send me newspaper articles he thought were interesting. We talked on the phone about once a week. I'd say, "Norris Baby, thank you so much for sending that article, blah, blah, blah…."

After I returned from Washington, I called Norris with an idea. "Norris Baby, I've been sharing my story. It's time we get yours on video tape. I'd like to fly down and make a video of the two of us talking about when you guys liberated us."

He agreed. I flew down to Florida to make a video about our experience. I hired a video professional who taped Norris and me chatting about the liberation. The video man put it all together with narration, music, and photos. It was our own documentary. We shake hands and hug at the end.

We made plans for Norris to travel to St. Louis. We were going to hold a nice event at the Holocaust Museum, but Norris' health kept him from coming. Sadly he passed away on August 12, 2011. He would have been 100 years old in October of 2011. I miss him. Every once in a while I watch the video we made, just to see him again.

Norris and I used to have some very good talks. He was a soft-spoken, gentleman. He wanted to know all about what the Germans had done to us in the camps. It made him angry, and sometimes it even moved him to curse (not something he'd usually do). He'd lost some very close friends battling the Germans across Europe, so he already carried that sorrow and anger. He told me that once he saw us on the road in Cham, however, he understood for the first time what the war was all about. It made it clear to him why their sacrifice was worthwhile.

Norris was a highly educated fellow. As a teenager he attended Philip Exeter Academy, which is among the finest private college preparatory schools in the country. He went on to obtain an Ivy League education at Dartmouth University. Isn't it amazing? I'm mostly self-educated: with only a few years formal education in grade school. On the other hand, Norris was educated at the very finest schools. I started life as a poor, Polish Jew. He came from a well-to-do Christian family in America.

How in the world could such different people, from different parts of the globe, end up becoming the best of friends? Our lives intersected briefly on that road outside Cham in 1945. Maybe we met each other? If we did, neither of us could remember. Then decades later we were old men living mere minutes from one another. We may have passed each other at the market a dozen times without knowing it.

Thank God Norris noticed the small article in our local paper, tracked me down through Rabbi Mendel's office, and made the call. Finally we not only ended up meeting, but eventually became great friends! God has an interesting way of weaving the cloth of our lives.

Keep this in mind as you go about your daily business. Someone you pass at the market today could end up being an important part of your life decades from now.

I think Norris was angrier at the Germans than I. The friends he lost died fighting, and that was hard enough a burden for him to carry. He mentioned to me on several occasions feeling a sense of guilt. He wondered why they died, and he survived. However what the Nazis had perpetrated upon people like me, the innocent and unarmed, especially angered him. I think that's why Norris was very curious about what I'd experienced in the camps and during the marches. That's how our wonderful American soldiers are wired. They have a big heart for the defenseless. Also perhaps knowing in detail about what I'd been through helped him to better understand just how evil his enemy was. It helped him to better understand what type of world we would have lived in, had the Allies lost. It may have given clear meaning to the ultimate sacrifice his brothers in arms had made.

I feel no ill will toward the Germans. I've never been back to Germany, but mainly because there are so many other places I've never been. I've never owned a German car, but only because I love America so much I can only drive American cars.

I've had the honor of meeting several of our local World War II veterans who liberated camps. The Holocaust Museum was doing a video project collecting interviews from liberators. There are some crazy people in the world these days who are claiming the Holocaust never happened, or that it wasn't as bad as they say. That's why I started giving talks about it. But the Holocaust deniers might just say, "Oh, the survivors like Ben Fainer are all Jews. They're all just making this stuff up." That's why the liberators' stories are very important. They saw the camps. Some were Jews, like Israel Friedman. Most weren't. Survivor testimony is powerful. Liberator testimony is also powerful. Together they are undeniable.

There were hundreds of camps and sub-camps all across Germany and Poland. At the end the Nazis were getting squeezed in from all sides. The British were invading from the north, the Americans from the south and west, and the Russians from the east. As the Allies were working their way toward Berlin, camps were being liberated here and there as the front lines moved inward.

I'd like to take you back again to my liberation. This time, however, I'd like to cover it from my liberators' point of view. As you may recall I was liberated by the 26th Infantry Division. The 26th was nicknamed the "Yankee Division" because most of the guys came from the area around New England. The nickname started back in World War I and continued into World War II. They all wore division patches on their uniforms with the letters "YD" for Yankee Division.

The 26th fought and helped defeat the Germans once during World War I, spending 210 days in combat, losing 1,587 men, and over 12,000 wounded.

They were called upon to fight the Germans once again in World War II. The 26th Infantry Division landed in France at Cherbourg and Utah Beach on September 7, 1944, just one day into the D-Day invasion. They fought their way across France, which included house-to-house fighting and pushed back the Germans during the Battle of the Bulge. They crossed the Rhine River on March 25.

The 26th received high praise for their efforts during the Battle of the Bulge from their commanding officer Willard S. Paul, Major General, Headquarters 26th Infantry Division. General Paul's letter of commendation included the following:

"When you initially attacked for seven days and nights without halting for rest, you met and defeated twice your own number. Your advance required the enemy to turn fresh divisions against you, and you in turn hacked them to pieces as you ruthlessly cut your way deep into the flank of the "bulge." Your feats of daring and endurance in sub-freezing weather and snow-clad mountains and gorges of Luxembourg are legion; your contribution to the relief of Bastogne was immeasurable. It was particularly fitting that the elimination of the "bulge" should find the Yankee Division seizing and holding firmly on the same line held by our own forces prior to the breakthrough. I am proud of this feat by you as well as those you performed earlier. We shall advance on Berlin together."

The general was proud of his soldiers, as he should have been. I read this, and it brought tears to my eyes. Can you imagine what these brave men had been through? These were not some guys you watch in a war movie. These were real people. These were my friends, Israel, Norris, and all the others. They were obviously fierce warriors: as battle-hardened as one can be. Yet many were brought to tears when they liberated us. They treated us with incredible compassion and kindness. It is a testament to the American soldier that he can possess such a heart – a heart capable of bringing hell upon an evil enemy and heaven upon the defenseless. The 26th reached us in the pouring rain at 10:00 a.m. in Cham, Germany on April 23.

Norris was in Company K of the 326th regiment, and here is a little bit of the two of us taken from the interview that was made into a video.

Norris: *"I am Norris Nimms, and I'm here to tell you how I met Ben Fainer. It was the morning of April 23, 1945, 10:00 a.m., when our division was attacking the town of Cham, Germany. As we approached the village from Swatzenberg, we entered the city over the bridge into the city itself. As we approached we saw this long group of captive people. As we liberated this large group, I could see they'd been through quite a bit of work and damage. It's not very often that a Liberator meets the person that he's liberated. I think it's quite a rare case that the two meet."*

Ben: *"And thanks to you and the American Forces that liberated us. And that's one of the reasons that I'm here today, and I thank you very, very much. And I hope to God that we never see such a horrifying thing, that I have seen, and what I went through. And thanks to soldiers like you that a lot of us are here today because of guys like you. And I want to thank you from the bottom of my heart. And I hope we live another hundred years. So you take good care my buddy and stay well. And my God keep you well."*

At that point in the interview Norris and I stand, shake hands, and hug. My daughter posted the video on the Internet. I'm not all that great with computers, but I've been told it's very easy to find by using Norris' name or mine.

Less than a week after my liberation, Norris was involved in a very dangerous assault on a heavily defended bridge. For his actions he was awarded the Bronze Star! Here is how his commanding officer described his valor on the official recommendation for the medal:
"PFC Norris G Nims while serving with the Army of the United States, distinguished himself by heroic achievement in connection with military operations against an armed enemy. During this Unit's attack in the vicinity of Kellberg, Germany on 1 May, 1945, PFC Norris G. Nims was a rifleman in Company K, 328th Infantry Regiment. The squad of which PFC Nims was a member was assigned the mission of taking and securing a bridge to be used by the Company in its advance over a tributary of the Danube River. In approaching the bridge into the town of Kellberg, PFC Nims and his companions encountered two

road blocks, both of which were defended by riflemen and machine guns. Despite the fire of enemy troops, he and his companions stormed the emplacements directly, taking all of the enemy prisoners. Continuing on and infiltrating over the bridge, he and his companions cleared the town of enemy troops, after which they established a PW enclosure and outposted the village. In this action PFC Nims and his companions took a total of 120 prisoners. PFC Nims was not wounded."

I'm speechless. Reading about his bravery has brought tears to my eyes and a chill up my spine. I'm so incredibly proud to have known such a man! I told you he was an incredible fella.

The 26th continued into Austria and then into Czechoslovakia. There, along with the 11th Armored Division, they liberated Gusen concentration camp. At Gusen they discovered a vast tunnel system the Germans had constructed using slave labor. The tunnels housed airplane production facilities protected from aerial bombing. The liberation prevented the SS officers at Gusen from a possible plan to demolish the tunnels with all the prisoners inside.

The 26th returned to the United States on December 21, 1945. All in all they spent 199 days in combat losing 1,678 men. Over 7,300 men were wounded, 740 missing in action, and 159 taken as prisoners of war. Adding up combat and non-combat, the total casualties for the 26th reached nearly 17,000. Their sacrifice helped to keep the world free. Their sacrifice set me free.

I've learned that in addition to using the village of Cham to treat survivors, the Americans brought P.O.W.s there as well. American P.O.W.s on a death-march from the slave labor camp of Berga, a notorious camp which held P.O.W.s, were liberated by the 11th Armored Division on April 22. The P.O.W.s were then brought to Cham. The 11th took over a building and converted it into a make-shift hospital.

The 11th Armored Division worked hand-in-hand with the 26th Infantry Division, as together they swept quickly across Germany. After they'd taken Cham, the tanks of the 11th led the way, with the soldiers of the 26th, including Norris, following directly behind. And, of course, on the morning of April 23 their progress was abruptly interrupted as the road was clogged as far as the eye could see by our column of prisoners. I've read several interviews of soldiers from both the 26th and 11th, which include descriptions of my liberation. Their accounts match those that Norris and I have provided nearly word-for-word: thousands of starving prisoners, many dying from gunshots to the head, chaotic joy upon liberation.

What can I tell you about these brave soldiers? I simply don't have the words in my vocabulary to describe what is in my heart. I'm so very proud to be an American. We Americans are so very lucky to have the finest young men and women in the world sacrificing to protect our freedom and helping the helpless of the world. I was once one of the helpless. Thanks to a gracious God in Heaven, and fine American soldiers, I'm free.

Chapter Twenty-Six

Dachau, Flossenbürg, & Gross-Rosen

I spent over six years moving from camp-to-camp before finally being liberated along the roadside in Cham. At about that same time, the Allies were encountering and liberating hundreds of other camps and sub-camps including the camps where I'd previously been imprisoned. I, as you may recall, was part of a death-march that originated at Dachau.

On April 29 Dachau concentration camp was liberated by soldiers from the 42nd Infantry Division: nicknamed the "Rainbow Division." I've had the pleasure and honor of meeting several of the soldiers who helped liberate Dachau. One soldier described being able to smell the camp from over a mile away. He said it was an unholy smell.

Another described coming upon a train full of prisoners that had arrived at the camp, but had not been unloaded. The soldiers searched car after car, all filled with dead prisoners, hoping to find anyone who'd survived. A great cheer broke out across the entire camp when they finally found a single survivor among the 1,500 dead.

Before Dachau I was a prisoner at Flossenbürg. I've learned that on April 20, 1945, probably the day I began the death-march out of Dachau, the SS had ordered the evacuation of Flossenbürg. There were 22,000 inmates in the death-march out of Flossenbürg. Only those too sick to walk were left behind. Along the way more than 7,000 died from exhaustion, starvation, and illness. Many were killed by gunshot.

On April 23, the same day I was liberated, troops from the 90th Infantry Division and 97th Infantry Division came upon death-march prisoners and liberated the camp at Flossenbürg. At the time of liberation only about 1,600 prisoners were found inside the camp at Flossenbürg. Their liberators uncovered German records indicating more than 30,000 inmates died at Flossenbürg during its horrible existence.

I was imprisoned at Gross-Rosen prior to Flossenbürg. As the Allies were closing in the Germans began the evacuation of the Gross-Rosen sub-camps as early as January 1945. Evacuation of the main camp began in February. Approximately 40,000 prisoners, 20,000 of which were Jews, were imprisoned at the main camp at that time.

Some were evacuated on open air cattle or coal cars to Bergen-Belsen, Buchenwald, Dachau, Flossenbürg, Mauthausen, Dora-Mittelbau, and Neurengamme. Many died on their way to these camps. Others were forced on death-marches. Soviet forces liberated Gross-Rosen on February 13, 1945. Approximately 40,000 prisoners died at the Gross-Rosen complex over its years of use. This estimate includes those who died on trains and marches during the evacuation effort.

Chapter Twenty-Seven

The Liberation of Buchenwald

I was held at Buchenwald prior to Gross-Rosen. Ohrdruf, a sub-camp of Buchenwald, was the very first camp liberated by American troops. It was liberated on April 4, 1945, by the U.S. 89th Infantry Division.

As I said I didn't stay at Ohrdruf, but rather the main camp of Buchenwald. I found out an amazing thing that took place at Buchenwald. Of course I didn't know about any of this at the time. There was a Polish prisoner there named Gwidon Damazyn who'd been there since 1941. He was an engineer and had somehow secretly built a radio transmitter and generator!

As the Allies were closing in, the Germans started marching large numbers of prisoners out from the camp. On April 9, 1945, Damazyn sent a message on his radio: *"To Allies. To General Patton's Army. This is concentration camp Buchenwald. S.O.S. We need help. They're trying to evacuate us. The SS try to exterminate us."*

They repeated the message four times, each time in English, Russian, and German. After about fifteen minutes, Damazyn heard an answer from the U.S. Third Army promising help as soon as they could get there! Can you imagine the joy this bright man must have felt?

What happened next was equally amazing. A bunch of Communist prisoners had somehow secretly stolen and hidden a machine gun and nearly 100 rifles. These prisoners must have lived under very different circumstances than I did at Buchenwald. Among those the Germans labeled as "undesirables," the Jews were the lowest of the low. They truly thought we were less than human deserving the harshest of treatment followed by death. Building the transmitter and amassing weapons would have been impossible in our section of the camp. We were lucky to be able to steal and hide a piece of wire to repair a shoe. Anything more than that would have been impossible.

As word about the radio message from the Americans quickly spread throughout the camp, the group of Communist prisoners used their stolen weapons to kill the remaining guards.

Elie Wiesel, Nobel Peace Prize winner and well known author of the book, "Night," was a prisoner of Buchenwald at the time of liberation. Wiesel, who was only a teenager, had been able to care for his father during their year or so in the camps. Sadly on January 29, 1945, Wiesel's ailing father was taken away to the Buchenwald crematorium facilities. As you know these were located just outside Block 15, the barracks I had stayed in. If only his father could have held out a couple more months, he may have survived.

The original crematorium facilities at Buchenwald are not the ones you see in photos today. I believe the ones that were outside Block 15 while I was there were actually mobile ovens made by Topf & Sons Company based in nearby Erfurt. These ovens were designed for use on farms for burning cattle cadavers and were later altered to better fit the dark needs of the SS. The original ovens were replaced in 1941 and again in 1942. These changes enclosed the ovens inside a building structure.

I've learned something else interesting about Buchenwald, and it also involved Flossenbürg. A German Lutheran pastor named Dietrich Bonhoeffer, who had been very active in resisting Hitler, had been a prisoner at Buchenwald. He was arrested by the Gestapo in 1943 and sent to Buchenwald. He was later sent to Flossenbürg. Sadly, just a little before liberation, he was executed by hanging for his role in an earlier plot to kill Hitler.

Troops of the U.S. 9th Armored Infantry Battalion, the U.S. 6th Armored Division, and the U.S. Third Army officially liberated Buchenwald on April 11th. They were given a hero's welcome. Some of

Silent for Sixty Years

the survivors, believe it or not, actually tossed the liberators into the air as a show of thanks and joy! These must have been non-Jewish prisoners, as Jewish prisoners would not have been in good enough shape to do so.

No one knows exactly how many people were killed or died over the years at Buchenwald: for some reason the Germans in charge there didn't register a significant number of prisoners. From what historians can tell, the SS murdered at least 56,000 male prisoners at Buchenwald and its sub-camps.

As I mentioned earlier, I've been trying to locate Israel Friedman's family. This is a daunting task as there are over 45 Israel Friedmans currently listed in Brooklyn! I'm calling each and every one, but so far I have not yet been successful. Even though I've yet to find my Israel's family, I'm making new friends on nearly every call! These total strangers have responded to my quest with open arms, even volunteering to start calling everyone they know with the last name of Friedman. I do hope to find Israel's family. I'd love to talk with his children and learn more about this wonderful man. I'm assuming that he's passed away, but you never know. The way life is, every time I dial the next phone number on my list, I half expect to hear the voice of my long lost friend on the other end.

I've recently located a letter written by a soldier named Israel Friedman to his wife back home. The letter, which describes what he observed after the liberation of Buchenwald, first appeared in a 1945 edition of "*The Signaleer*," a publication of the U.S. Army Signal Corps. This Israel Friedman, like my Israel Friedman, was a staff sergeant in the U.S. Army Signal Corps. And this Israel, like my Israel, arrived at Buchenwald just after its liberation. So I can't tell you with 100% certainty that my Israel was the author of the letter. But even if there happen to have been two Israel Friedmans, who were staff sergeants in the Signal Corp, and who both arrived at Buchenwald right after its liberation, I believe my Israel Friedman wrote this letter. I think this because the style of his writing reads very much the way he spoke with me back in Cham.

A Letter from Buchenwald, 1945
By Israel Friedman

Dear Alice:

By the time your letter reached me, I had moved all the way across France and a good part of Germany. What changes will have taken place between today, in the midst of so many peace rumors, and the day you get this letter?....

Enclosed you will find an account of our last assignment...an experience that without doubt was the most terrible I ever encountered---or expect to....

You know the horrors that were found at Buchenwald. By this time you've read all the stories of the piles of bodies found outside the crematory; you've seen the pictures of the heaps of bones; you've heard the commentators describe the remains found at Buchenwald, in the furnaces, and tell of the lampshades made of human skin. They're all true. But how can words and pictures alone properly convey the suffering that existed?....

51,000 people, perhaps more, died here. Did I say died? Not exactly. They were burned to death here, they were hanged to death here, they were mischievously shot to death here. Many, many thousands were kept at the threshold of death, suffering illness, hunger and acute torture until dying was a welcome thing.

Day and night the smoke could be seen rising from the chimneys of the crematory, and the fuel used was not always dead....

It is important to remember that Buchenwald was only one of Hitler's many horror resorts. Those that have since been liberated, and those still to be liberated, will prove to be worse in every respect. But in them, we may hope to find the people on whom Germany's future will depend.

I've included the above letter just as it appeared in the Signal Corps publication. Israel visited Buchenwald and wrote this letter to his wife several weeks before befriending me in Cham. His descriptions of Buchenwald mirror my own, particularly when he writes about live people being burned in the crematory. I do hope to locate Israel's family. I wonder if they have any more of his letters. I wonder if any mention me.

Chapter Twenty-Eight

Blechhammer & Bergen-Belsen

As you'll recall my first two camps, the temporary slave labor camp in Jeleśnia and Blechhammer concentration camp, were both in Poland. The Russians liberated the camps in Poland as they advanced toward Germany.

While I was at Blechhammer, I didn't know it was part of the much larger Auschwitz system of camps. I've since learned it was a satellite camp of Auschwitz. Early on, maybe while I was there, it was a separate camp. It was later brought under the umbrella of the Auschwitz system. Blechhammer was located a little less than 50 miles from the main camp of Auschwitz.

I've learned there were two plants near Blechhammer that produced synthetic oil. By June of 1944, the U.S. Air Force listed these plants as vital targets. By the end of the war, the 15th Air Force had dropped over 7,000 tons of bombs in the area of Blechhammer

In October of 1944 Heinrich Himmler ordered the destruction of the crematorium facilities at the camps within the Auschwitz system. He was trying to hide the atrocities he'd unleashed upon millions of innocent people. The SS blew up the gas chambers at Birkenau in January of 1945. Birkenau was the death camp of the Auschwitz sys-

150

tem. It is where my dear mother may have been murdered. As I mentioned records have recently turned up indicating Hannah Urman was alive at Auschwitz in 1944. Although I have my doubts, I'm still working to find out it these records are accurate.

I think it is very likely my siblings were murdered shortly after leaving Bedzin. At that time the Germans had just invaded Poland. The gas chambers and crematorium facilities had not yet been built. I can only guess that they were probably shot and buried some place in a mass grave. Maybe my dear mother was killed along with her children. Or, if the records are correct, she spent five or more years surviving in the camps. It pains my heart to think my mother may have actually witnessed her own children, including her newborn baby, being murdered. My mother was the queen of mothers. She was so incredibly kind... I don't have the vocabulary to describe how great she was.

I saw many unspeakable acts in the camps and on the marches. The brutality was horrific. If you weren't there, and I'm so glad that you were not, you have no way to imagine what it was like. But nothing, absolutely nothing, I experienced could have possibly been worse than my mother having her children ripped from her arms and murdered before her eyes. I hope to God it didn't happen that way. I think I would have begged them to shoot me right there and then.

But my mother was as strong as she was kind. Maybe she somehow willed herself to get through each day. Maybe she did this hoping to someday find me? I'll never know. But to tell you the truth, even during all my years of silence, when I didn't talk to anyone about the camps, I wondered about this. Only God knows. But I know one thing for sure. I took after my mother. I got her strength, and I think I got her good heart. You'll have to ask the people who know me about the heart. You know, because how can you judge your own heart? I think I never gave up in the camps because I inherited her strength.

And you know about my father. I guess I could thank him that I got his size, as being big for my age kept me from being sent off to die with the women and children. I think in a strange way he prepared me to survive in the camps. I learned from a very early age not to do anything that might set him off, not to give him even half a reason to slap me down. I was in constant fear of him; so I learned to keep my mouth shut, to blend into the background, and to do my work. These were all vital skills for surviving among kapos and SS men. Lastly he was a fine tailor, a real craftsman. I don't like to brag, but I was too.

On January 17, 1945, about 60,000 prisoners were evacuated from the Auschwitz camps. They were either marched or transported in cattle cars toward Germany. Only people who were too sick or too weak were left behind. On that same day, the SS command sent orders for all the remaining prisoners in the Auschwitz system to be executed. But in the chaos of making a quick retreat, the orders were never carried out. The 322nd Rifle Division of the Red Army liberated 7,500 prisoners at Auschwitz on January 27, 1945.

About 20,000 Auschwitz prisoners survived the death-march and death-trains and made it all the way to Bergen-Belsen in Germany. This was the camp I visited after liberation during my search for surviving relatives. You'll remember the Germans abandoned Bergen-Belsen days before liberation in April of 1945, leaving the prisoners without food or water.

Blechhammer was mostly evacuated on January 21, 1945, with prisoners heading toward Germany on death-marches and death-trains. It was liberated by the Red Army on January 28, 1945. I was not able to find out the number of prisoners who died or were killed at Blechhammer. However I did learn the death rate was estimated to be almost 86%.

Chapter Twenty-Nine

Jeleśnia and Bedzin

Still following my path backward, you'll recall that before I was taken to Blechhammer, my father and I were held for months at a camp in Jeleśnia, Poland. The Germans had just invaded Poland two days before we were taken from our apartment in Bedzin and brought to the camp at Jeleśnia.

The Polish Army had been no match for the invading German forces. However I've learned Polish forces fought with great skill in a number of battles. During the invasion 60,000 Polish soldiers were killed, 6,000 of whom were Jewish.

I haven't been able to find out very much about the camp in Jeleśnia. I've even been told by some "experts" that there wasn't a camp there. Well, I'm no expert, but I beg to differ. I was there. Why would I make that up?

I have a guess as to why there's no information about a camp at Jeleśnia. I think it was only a temporary camp used to hold us while the real camps were being constructed. I've learned there was a Polish Army fort at Jeleśnia that was still under construction at the time of the German invasion. It was called *152 Kompania Forteczna Jeleśnia* (152 Company Fortress Jeleśnia). The 152 was a sub-unit of the Polish First Mountain Brigade. The camp had not been entirely completed at the time Poland was invaded. I think the Germans quickly converted the Polish fort into our temporary camp.

Maybe nothing was written about the forced labor camp at Jeleśnia because by the time the war ended, it hadn't been used to hold prisoners for over five years. There was no liberation for the Soviet Army to document; it was just an old empty Polish Army fort. Also I read the Germans may have stripped it of anything useful for use elsewhere. If you travel to Jeleśnia today, there's nothing left of our wooden barracks. There are only a couple of crumbling defensive bunkers to show there was ever a Polish Army fort.

I also learned about a notable event that happened in Jeleśnia during the war. An American B-24 Liberator bomber ended up crash landing there on September 13, 1944. The plane was named "The Dinah Might." It was part of a mission to bomb the I.G. Farben factories near Auschwitz. Among the many things I.G. Farben produced to support the war effort, it also owned the patent for the pesticide Zyklon B. This was the chemical used to kill prisoners in the gas chambers. A monument has been erected in the area to honor the mission.

Finally we're back to where it all started: my home town of Bedzin, Poland. The war itself appears to have begun in the German border town of Gleiwitz, which is just a little due west of Bedzin. On August 31, 1939, the Gestapo dressed a prisoner from a homeland concentration camp in a Polish Army uniform and shot him outside the local radio station in Gleiwitz. This, which became known as the Gleiwitz deception, was a hoax perpetrated in order to make the false claim that the Polish had attacked Germany. When the Germans began their invasion of Poland the following morning, Hitler cited the Polish attack on the Gleiwitz transmitter as one of his justifications for the action.

Seven months earlier, while speaking in Berlin, Hitler had been very straight forward about his plans for the Jews. If war broke out, "The result will not be the Bolshevization of the earth, and thus the victory of Jewry, but the annihilation of the Jewish race in Europe."

What happened after the *Wehrmacht* (regular German Army) swept through the area and took us away in 1939? The *Wehrmacht* was followed by the *Einsatzruppen*, which translates from German into "task forces." Their task was to murder Jews. They were SS paramilitary squads responsible for mass killings: usually by gunshot.

They would kill Jews and other groups marked as "undesirables" by the Nazi regime.

The *Einsatzruppen* followed German invading forces killing undesirables as they were encountered. Sometimes an operation would involve the murder of a few. In heavily populated areas it could go on for days. Examples of this are the infamous massacre at Babi Yar, in which they murdered nearly 34,000 people in two days and the Rumula massacre, where they killed 25,000 people in two days. In total the *Einsatzruppen* murdered over 1,000,000 people. They swept through Bedzin in September of 1939. On September 8 several hundred Jews were locked inside the synagogue, and the building was set on fire. All were burned alive. This was my synagogue. It is where my mother's father was a rabbi. It is where my baby sister would have received her name. It is where I likely would have been a rabbi had it not been for that Godless monster, Hitler.

As needed for labor, the Germans rounded up able working males from Bedzin. In March of 1941, 5,000 Jewish men of Bedzin were taken to work in the coal fields in the Upper Silesian region.

Jews fleeing persecution in western Poland flocked into Bedzin, hoping to find refuge. Thus the Jewish population doubled during that time of trouble. At first the people of Bedzin didn't know where the Germans were taking Jews. Most believed Jews were being resettled elsewhere. In 1942 a woman somehow escaped from Auschwitz and made her way back to Bedzin. She told people about Auschwitz, and they believed her. This was not always the case. There were other rare cases of escapees returning to warn their hometown people, but they were not believed. The stories were too incredible for the people to accept. Word spread throughout Bedzin, and many people began building secret hiding places in their dwellings.

The Germans created a Jewish ghetto in Bedzin during May of 1942. Over 20,000 Jews from Bedzin were imprisoned within the ghetto, as well as an additional 10,000 Jews who'd been displaced from the surrounding area. Initially most were forced to work at local factories. Over time the Germans initiated a series of deportations, transporting large numbers of Jews to camps within the Auschwitz system for immediate extermination or forced labor, depending on age and health.

During the final major deportation effort in August of 1943, a Bedzin Ghetto chapter of the Jewish Combat Organization (Ż.O.B.)

attempted to instigate an uprising in defiance of the Germans. The uprising was an extremely brave effort. However most of the Jewish fighters were killed by overwhelming German forces.

Historians estimate that of the 30,000 Jewish prisoners of the Bedzin Ghetto, only 2,000 survived. A memorial to the Bedzin Ghetto was dedicated in 2005. Over 250 of my relatives were murdered during the Holocaust. I'll never know how each of them died. Whether one of my cousins died in the ghetto, in a camp, or on a march isn't important. What is important is that you realize that each was a real person, with real hopes and dreams. Please don't become overwhelmed by the numbers: thousands, tens of thousands, millions. I was one who survived. You know my story. These people had their own stories, which were tragically cut short. It's very important to think of each as an actual person: a brother, sister, husband or wife.

Chapter Thirty

People and Dreams

At first I gave one or two talks a month. That soon became one or two a week. Earlier this week, I had my first triple-header – 3 talks in one day! Does it get easier? No and yes. No, it is still very difficult, very painful. And yes, I think with practice I'm getting better and better. And yes, I get to meet incredible, wonderful people.

I meet people of all ages. Of course I adapt how much of the horror I go into when I'm speaking with children. But I don't hold back too much either. They understand more than we give them credit for. I also speak quite often to older people at nursing homes. Often times the best questions come from the very young and the very old.

I speak to people of all faiths and races. History is long. Nearly every group on the planet has suffered at the hands of a brutal oppressor at some point or another. Everyone understands. They know it's happened to their people before. We all fear it will happen again.

Something special happens when I tell my story to a group. I'm sure this is true for the other survivors as well. A bond is formed. I don't know exactly how or why, but it happens each and every time. It's a long and horrible story. Perhaps, by the time I finish, the people feel like they've been through it with me?

A close friend, a father of two boys, told me how the story hit him. He said the story makes him mourn for the little boy I never got to be. That's how it hits him as a father. Maybe it hits other parents and grandparents the same way.

I don't know. I guess I can't. But I can tell you how bonding with all these wonderful people hits me. That is, I can try to put it into words. I can see a connection happening while I'm telling my story. I can see it in their eyes and in the expressions on their faces. It comes out further during questions. The bond is very strong immediately after, with the hugs and many, many kind words. It continues days later when I open the thank you notes from the adults and brightly colored drawings from the children.

To make all these meaningful connections, day-after-day, is a blessing beyond measure. But it comes at a cost. In the years after the camps, I had many nightmares. Over time they'd come only once or twice a year. However the more I talk, the more frequent they come.

Very rarely do I have bad dreams about the camps. As you know, the camps were living nightmares, but they were not the worst I suffered by far. My uttermost horror was the loss of my dear mother. Every night when my head hits the pillow, I brace myself for what might come. I tell myself not to worry. The bad dreams may come, but they're not real. The hugs from the people, these are real.

The nightmares come in many variations, but all have the same general setting and theme. I am back in my hometown of Bedzin before the trouble. They all start off wonderful, but end in terror. In one version I'm coming in from fetching the water. I'm freezing, but the apartment is warm. My mother warms me in her strong arms. In another I'm playing with my little brother and sister, while my mother cooks dinner. In yet another I'm helping my mother go to market: pulling our little cart, chatting with her, and greeting relatives and neighbors. The dreams are incredibly real. I wish you could control dreams. I'd stop the terror from coming. I'd will myself to stay asleep for hours and hours soaking up our life before the trouble. I'd eat bowl after bowl of my dear mother's goulash.

I refuse to share the details of what happens when the dreams turn bad. I will say only that they involve the SS and play out in horrible detail. I will say only that they involve the very worst fears of what may have happened to my mother and siblings. And the bad parts often include the screaming…the screaming of those poor live souls being push into the ovens outside Block 15. I wish you could control dreams.

Chapter Thirty-One

Work Sets You Free

The Nazis murdered approximately six million Jews. It is estimated that of the 3.3 million Jews of pre-war Poland, only 300,000 survived. The Nazis killed another seven million Soviet prisoners of war and civilians in concentration camps, along with 500,000 people belonging to the so-called "gypsy" groups, and 80,000 sick and handicapped people of German origin. These numbers are too massive to understand.

It's easy to forget that these were real people with real lives and dreams that were taken from them. Now you know a little bit about one person who survived. And you know about my dear mother, my brother Majer, my sister Rosie, and my baby sister. What would Majer have become? What of the children and grandchildren Rosie may have had? And the baby, at least the baby could have had a name.

How could this happen in a modern European nation in the 20th century? I don't believe there is anything uniquely dark within the souls of the German people. I've met many people from many different places and cultures around the world. I think deep down we are all the same. We all have an enormous capacity for kindness. We all have an enormous capacity for hatred. You don't' need to have survived the Holocaust to know this. Simply watch the evening news, where nightly you see true human nature, both good and bad, played out here and there across the globe. Then get up every morning and ask yourself, "Who will I be today?"

You may think, "This could never happen here, not in the United States of America." I pray you're right, but I must scold you a little for this way of thinking. If you think it could never happen here, you may wish to do a little reading about American history. Like I've said, this is the greatest country in the world. I'm very proud to be a U.S. citizen. However I've read a little about slavery. I've read a little about what we did to the American Indians. These were a long time ago. We've learned from our past errors. I hope we never make such terrible mistakes again. But let's not take any chances. As the saying goes, never say never.

I've been speaking about the Holocaust for about four years now. I want people to know that it could happen here, but only if we let it. How do we guard against it? The first step is to never forget the Holocaust, and never forget the other genocides that have happened and still happen.

We also must protect our wonderful system of government. It has become our national past-time to criticize our government. I've heard a saying, "Our system of government is the worst in the world, except for all the others." Don't be fooled by all this. It's just a fashionable thing to say. Our system is the best. Yes, we make mistakes. Yes, we've done some horrible things. But we are not defined by our mistakes. I'd like to think we learn from them, and we're improving over time.

For instance it was wrong to imprison Japanese-Americans during World War II. We didn't make the same mistake in regard to Muslim-Americans after 911. We have great hearts. We do a great deal of good; I think far, far more than bad. We may go temporarily astray, but we always find our way back home. It is our job – no – your job to stand guard, to call foul when we go astray, and to help us find our way back. "What can I do?" you may ask. We live in a free country with elected leaders and a free press. Call your elected representatives. Write a letter to your local newspaper. Vote at each and every election. Anyone can sit on the sidelines and complain about how things ought to be. I tell you just what I'd sometimes tell such guys in the camps, "Shut up. Stop worrying. Get to work."

We can learn to protect our system by looking at what Hitler did. He didn't start off saying he would become a brutal dictator bent on world domination and mass murder. The Germans gave him his power bit-by-bit. They allowed him to turn one group of people against another. They grew drunk on his promises of national greatness.

So we must not give a leader more power than he or she is entitled in our constitution. That is pretty simple. Next we must be tolerant of people. Everyone should be treated fairly under our laws. You don't have to agree with someone. You don't have to practice what they do or what they think. But you should treat people with respect. That is pretty simple. I'm not a philosopher. I'm not an expert in these matters. I'm a tailor.

I heard on the news that the First Lady of our great nation was recently booed while she attended a baseball game. This is an example of what I'm talking about. You may not agree with her politics, but please show her respect. Show her position respect. Don't believe all that the right or left say about their own guys, nor what they say about the other side. I promise you their guys aren't as good as they say. The other side's guys are not as evil as they say. Don't believe all the hogwash. Use the wonderful brain Almighty God has given you. Listen to both sides. Learn to pick bits of truth from within the manure.

We are all Americans. Our system of government is designed for constant disagreement. It's messy, but it's a good thing. I want an America where no one person or party gets too much power. So please, please be passionate about your political beliefs whatever side you're on. Join the mess. Jump in with both feet. Just don't make the mistake of believing that the other side is evil. Sometimes your side will get its way. Sometimes it will not. This is a wonderful thing.

It is great to be proud of your political beliefs. Yet it is better to approach this with a healthy amount of humility. We're not playing a football game here; peoples' lives are in the balance. Cheer for your side, but don't lose your objectivity. It's very unlikely the theories of one side will be right, all the time, in every situation.

Imagine three golfers playing a round of golf. One guy says, "It's all about the drive. I'm using my driver on every shot." The second says, "No, it's all about putting. I'm using my putter on every shot. The third says, "Driving is very important. Putting also is very important. I've got a whole bag full of clubs. I will use whichever club is the best for each shot." Who would you bet on?

If you disagree, please understand. I lost my dear mother, my siblings, and over 250 relatives because one side became too strong. The people grew drunk with one party's power. The people believed the other people were evil. This doesn't happen overnight. It's a slow, insidious process. We don't want to go down that road. It leads to the very worst in us. We have a really good thing going here in America. Let's not mess it up.

I speak to groups of every race, religion, age…whatever. I speak in the morning, during the day, and late in the evening. Just as I worked hard to stay alive in the camps, and I worked so hard for my family, now I work hard at this.

I often speak to young people. I tell them to work hard. Work hard at everything. Hard work can overcome a lot of problems. I came out of the camps an uneducated,70-pound kid, who'd been through the very worst life can throw at you. I could have said, "Life's not fair. I'm a victim. I give up."

I went to work and never stopped. I worked hard to learn to read, write, and speak English. I worked hard to learn a trade. I worked hard to provide for my family. I worked hard to be a good husband and father. And I worked very hard to enjoy life along the way.

I tell the kids not to let their problems define who they are. Everyone has problems. This is a tough world. No one gets off scot-free. Whatever baggage you're carrying around, hard work can make your life better. However, hard work can't make your life perfect though. "Perfect" doesn't exist.

I also tell them not to get overwhelmed by all the problems in the world. This is easy to do, especially for this generation. With television and the Internet they see every problem going on in the world played over and over again, 24 hours a day, seven days a week. For my generation life was different. For the most part we only saw the trouble that was right in front of us. There's a good Yiddish proverb that I share with them, "If each one sweeps before his own door, the whole street is clean." In other words, take care of your own troubles. That's how we make a better world.

I also speak to groups of soldiers. Sometimes I invite a group to the St. Louis Holocaust Museum. Other times I speak on-base. I've had the pleasure of speaking at Scott Air Force Base, in Illinois and

Fort Leonard Wood Army Base, in Missouri. I've loved meeting all these fine people, each and every one.

Of course they know a little bit about hard work, so I don't lecture them on that so much. I mostly give them my thanks. They are an important part of keeping us free. We owe them our respect and our thanks. I urge you to thank every soldier you see. Thank veterans too. They'll get embarrassed, but don't let that stop you. Thank them anyway.

I tell the soldiers about the wonderful soldiers who sacrificed so much to liberate me. I tell them about Norris. I want them to understand that they're changing the lives of the people they encounter in foreign lands. I say, "You never know. The little kid you meet in some God forsaken village someplace will grow up to be a man. Will he grow up hoping to one day come to America for a better life, just like I did? Or will he grow up wanting to visit America with a bomb strapped to his chest? You're not just doing a job out there. You're changing lives. I'm living proof."

After touring our museum and listening to my talk, a young soldier who'd seen his share of combat shared this with me, "I've only been in the presence of evil twice in my life. Once was in combat. The other was when I visited Auschwitz."

Another had this to say, "It's so hard to imagine. You hear about it and try to put yourself in your place. You ask yourself, 'How would I have survived?'"

Recently William M. Fraser, III, a four-star general and commander at Scott Air Force Base, brought a large group to the museum. General Fraser addressed his soldiers saying, "I'm so grateful Ben told me about this special place and invited us here today. We must do everything we can do to make sure this never happens again. That's why you volunteered; you signed up. There are a lot of extremists out there. The soldiers here today have the duty to go back to the base and tell others. I put forth this challenge to all of you. Tell this story. Tell people Ben's story and about this fine museum."

Recently I was invited to speak at the St. Louis office of the F.B.I. . I had to undergo a background check because, you know since 911, not just anyone can waltz into the offices of the F.B.I. . I joked a little with the officer in charge of the background check saying, "I guess I can't bring my pearl handled pistols with me?" Thankfully the officer understood my sometimes strange sense of humor. I passed the background check with flying colors.

I don't have the words in my vocabulary to describe these wonderful and incredible men and women at the F.B.I.! I spent five hours meeting everyone, even the big shots in charge, giving my talk and being shown around. These fine people make me so proud to be an American. I strongly believe it is no accident the terrorists have failed to hit our homeland again. If you ever meet someone with the F.B.I., I beg you to thank them for their service.

They invited me back to talk with another group the very next day. Best of all they invited me to a special dinner, where they made me an honorary member of the F.B.I.! How about that? Not bad for a poor kid from Bedzin, Poland!

At all my talks I ask everyone to be kind to the elderly. The little old man in front of you in line at the neighborhood deli, who might be taking longer than you'd like to place his order, may have parachuted behind enemy lines the night before the D-Day invasion at Normandy Beach. I've met such a hero here in St. Louis, a man named Phil Mc-Knight. He also liberated a Nazi camp. If you passed him at the grocery store, you'd never guess he helped push the Germans back at the Battle of the Bulge. If you took a moment to get to know him, you'd come away a better person. If you asked him what he would tell someone who was denying the Holocaust, you'd hear him say in his folksy, Southern Missouri accent, "I'd tell 'em they was crazy. I know it. I seen it!"

In Poland life was slower. We had more respect for our elders. Life is great here in America. It's the best place in the world, so I'm not saying we should live like I did back in Bedzin. I just think you're missing something if you don't take the time to talk with the older people around you. I practice what I'm preaching. I frequently give talks at area retirement centers. During question and answer, and after the talk, I learn quite a bit from these fine older people.

Another thing I tell people is that I'm not an island. You have to be strong and work hard in life, but you shouldn't try and do it all on your own. I could never have survived the camps, had it not been for the wonderful guys around me. I've lived this way every day since the camps. Every one of us is surrounded by wonderful people who need our friendship and help. You need their friendship and help. Give first without even thinking of getting back. It's an investment made in faith.

This is not just to the people close to you. It could be the old man sitting next to you in a deli. You could say hello. It could lead to a little chat. The chat could lead to a friendship. I've experienced this many times. Trust me. I've met amazing people this way. Or you could just ignore him, eat your sandwich, and rush off to get home in time to watch some singing competition on TV. It's up to you.

As you know I kept silent about the Holocaust for a long time. Sometimes people ask me if talking about it has helped me. It has, but not in the way most people think. It hasn't helped to ease the pain. Talking about it is hard. I don't enjoy it. My eyes still get wet when I talk about my dear mother. I talk about all this because I believe it is very important.

Do I have any regrets? Yes. We, I mean we survivors, should have talked about this as soon as we were liberated. We opened up this can of worms way too late. If we'd started telling our stories and warning people about this, maybe other genocides could have been avoided? Maybe the holocaust deniers wouldn't have sprouted up? We'll never know. I don't lose sleep over this, though. What's done is done. I can't change the past. All I can do is keep doing what I'm doing, talking to anyone and everyone who will listen. I will do this until my last breath.

Breaking my silence has made me a different person. I think I'm becoming a much better person. Before, I led a pretty sheltered life. I worked, and I spent time with my family. I didn't have time for much else. The people I've met while speaking have all been wonderful. I've yet to meet a single unpleasant person. They come eager to listen. They ask great questions. At the end I'm engulfed by handshakes and hugs.

I think a special bond is formed as we share the story of what I experienced. When I started writing this I expressed doubts that this could happen when someone simply reads my story. I hope something special happened, even if it's not quite the same as talking with me about it in person. While I plan on living to be 100, or maybe more, at some point all of the Holocaust survivors will be gone. All that will be left will be our words. I hope they will be enough.

Other regrets? Well, one – along the lines of what I was just discussing. I wish you didn't have to read my story. I wish I could have talked to you in person right here at my kitchen table. We could have had a couple drinks: Scotch for me and whatever you prefer for you. I could have cooked some of my famous home-made potato pancakes or chicken soup. Everyone tells me they're pretty darn good. I think in person, I could better help you understand. Best of all, I would have gotten to know you. I'm truly sorry about missing out on that.

"So what's next for me?" Ah…, that's a question just like the guys in the camps would always ask. Only God knows. What's next? I have no clue. I'm just going to keep working.

Photo Section Begins on the Following Page

Words In Praise of "Silent for Sixty Years" on Page 188

The only surviving photo of Ben, Rosie, and Majer Fainer.

Postcard showing Bedzin's castle and synagogue.

Several hundred Jews were locked inside the synagogue
in Bedzin. The building was set on fire and all were burned alive.

Modrizejowska Street, Bedzin, Poland.

German soldiers at Jeleśnia, Poland.

Bunker at 152 Company Fortress Jeleśnia.

Marker honoring American B-24 Liberator bomber, Jeleśnia.

Gate and tower at Blechhammer.

Barracks at Blechhammer.

The gate at Buchenwald.

Prisoners in bunks at Buchenwald.

The gate at Gross-Rosen.

Fences at Gross-Rosen.

Flossenbürg.

Unusual crematorium at Flossenbürg.

The gate at Dachau.

Work will set you free sign.

Prisoners on a Nazi death-march.

26th Army Infantry in Cham, Germany.

U.S. Flag flying over Buchenwald after liberation.

During Ben's recovery, his liberators dressed him in a
U.S. Army uniform for this photo.

Ben's Aunt Ida in Dublin, Ireland.

Controversial document listing Ben's mother
being at Auschwitz in 1944.

Ben's dear wife Susan Christina O'Brien Fainer.

Norris Nims, Ben's friend and liberator.

Ben's friend, liberator Norris Nims.

Best friends: liberator Norris Nims and Ben Fainer.

Ben speaking with a group of teens. Photo courtesy of Mike Sherwin, *The Jewish Light*.

Marci Rosenberg, Ben Fainer, and William M. Fraser, III,
Four-star General and Commander of Scott Air Force Base.
Photo courtesy of Mike Sherwin, *The Jewish Light*.

Ben Fainer, and William M. Fraser, III,
Four-star General and Commander of Scott Air Force Base.
Photo courtesy of Mike Sherwin, *The Jewish Light*.

Ben speaking with a group of soldiers.
Photo courtesy of Mike Sherwin, *The Jewish Light*.

Ben with WWII liberator Rev. Bob Weiss, S.J. .

Ben with friend and co-author Mark Leach.

Ben at the St. Louis Holocaust Museum & Learning Center.

About the Authors

Ben Fainer

After surviving six horrific years in Nazi camps, Ben went on to live a rich and fascinating life. He currently lives in St. Louis, Missouri. Ben enjoys spending time with his children, grandchildren, and great-grandchildren. Nearly every day, he speaks to various groups about his experience.

Mark Leach

Mark lives in Chesterfield, Missouri with his wife and two sons. He works in the pharmaceutical industry, but also is involved in a variety of volunteer activities, which often include writing. He met Ben while conducting a series of video interviews of local survivors and WWII liberators for the St. Louis Holocaust Museum & Learning Center.

Words of Praise for "Silent for Sixty Years"

"His words come from the heart and communicate the deeply felt emotions of a man who kept his humanity intact in spite of the inhumane situations he endured." Jean Cavender, Director, St. Louis Holocaust Museum & Learning Center.

"No one can ever understand the pain a survivor feels as they retell and relive the horror. I am thankful that Ben has decided to share his story with the world. He is a great man, and his mother would be very proud." Marci Levison Rosenberg, Shoah Foundation Interviewer, Past Chair, St. Louis Holocaust Museum & Learning Center.

"Not often am I moved by words alone. It's people like Ben who make our society better. Kindness and perseverance will overcome evil everytime." Michael Staenberg, President, THF Realty.

"Although you may have seen horrible pictures of Holocaust victims, you will experience a new and soul-searing appreciation of a terrible blot on human history from this simple, true, riveting account by a survivor." Rev. Robert F. Weiss, S.J., WWII Liberator – 42nd Rainbow Division, Former President of St. Louis University High School and Rockhurst University.

CPSIA information can be obtained
at www.ICGtesting.com
Printed in the USA
LVHW080121070521
686754LV00013B/841